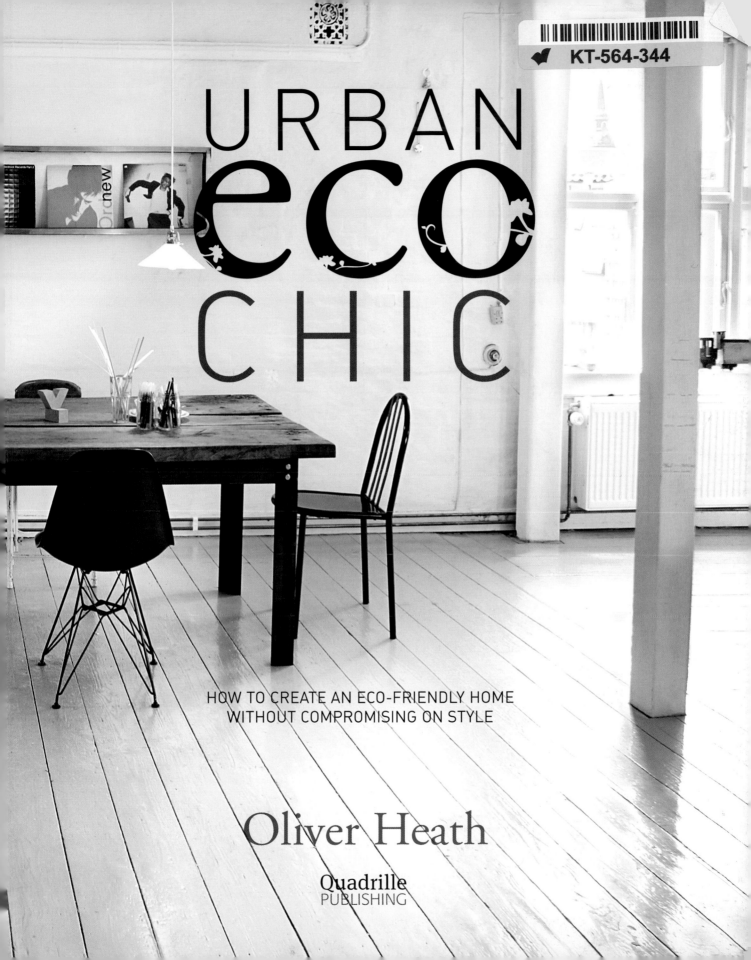

URBAN
eco
CHIC

HOW TO CREATE AN ECO-FRIENDLY HOME
WITHOUT COMPROMISING ON STYLE

Oliver Heath

Quadrille
PUBLISHING

For my girls, Katie, Lyla and Ottilie.
For whom a beautiful and sustainable future is so worthwhile.

Mixed Sources
Product group from well-managed
forests and other controlled sources
www.fsc.org   Cert no. SGS-COC-003963
© 1996 Forest Stewardship Council

FSC

All materials used in this book are
FSC certified.

Editorial Director Jane O'Shea
Creative Director Helen Lewis
Project Editor Lisa Pendreigh
Designer Claire Peters
Picture Researchers Helen Stallion &
Samantha Rolfe
Production Director Vincent Smith
Production Controller Ruth Deary

This paperback edition first published in 2010 by
Quadrille Publishing Limited
Alhambra House
27–31 Charing Cross Road
London WC2H 0LS
www.quadrille.co.uk

Text © 2008 Oliver Heath
Design and layout © 2008 Quadrille Publishing Limited

The rights of the author have been asserted.

Cataloguing in Publication Data: a catalogue record for
this book is available from the British Library.

ISBN: 978 184400 823 0

Printed in China

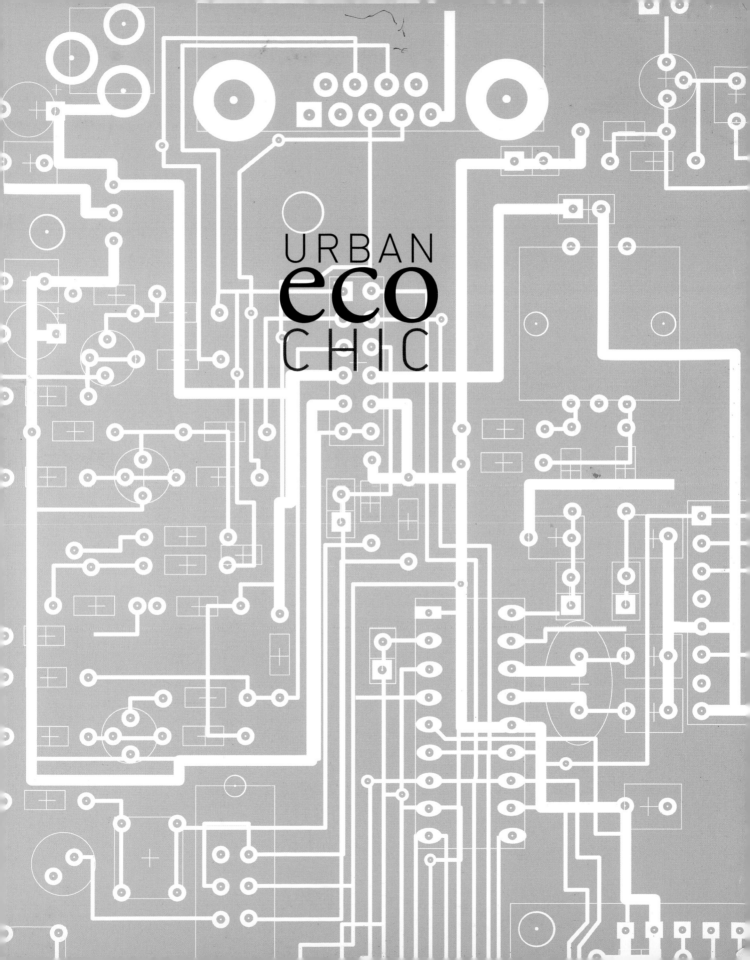

URBAN
eco
CHIC

As an interior designer, I feel a responsibility to do all I can to highlight the issue of climate change and the effect it is having on our lives and homes. The world we inhabit is changing due to our activities and as it changes we must adapt our lifestyles to compensate. I am not interested in relaying messages of doom and destruction, nor do I wish to layer on guilt to shame people into changing their ways. I prefer to take on board the facts of climate change and embrace a way of living that reduces my impact on the environment, but at the same time allows my home to be stylish and comfortable. After all, I am a designer who wants things to be just so – for form, function and sustainability go hand in hand.

My passion for eco design comes from a number of threads. A childhood spent playing on Brighton beach and in Sussex woodlands led to a fascination for nature. But it was when I became a windsurfing instructor aged 18 that I learnt to respect nature. Teaching others about the dangers we face when we take nature's power for granted gave me more experience – and scars – than I ever intended. We humans often forget how we are part of the natural world rather than set apart from it. Studying architecture for six years allowed me to combine my passion for nature with the built environment, exploring how our homes can work in tandem with nature rather than struggle against it.

Working in interior design, I am committed to finding ways of reducing our eco impact without compromising on style – to create a home that benefits both us and the environment. When I say benefits us, I mean it will cost less to run, be more comfortable to live in, contain fewer toxins and be a nurturing, comforting, inspiring place to call home. My aim is to make sustainable interiors accessible yet aspirational, without being overly expensive.

Over a number of years, I have accumulated my ideas on eco design and this book has provided an exciting opportunity to gather them together. My television design work offers invaluable experience in creating homes that reflect the character of the owners. My writing work for

Friends of the Earth and the *Observer*, and role as spokesperson for environmental groups such as the Energy Savings Trust, affords the opportunity to research sustainable practices and materials. Whilst private commissions for a variety of environmental groups, such as Bio Regional, offer the chance to put my eco designs into practice.

Most important – and closest to my heart – is my own eco home. On moving into a mid-nineteenth-century townhouse, I seized the opportunity to carry out a largely sustainable refurbishment; my goal was to create a beautiful, inspiring home with minimal environmental impact. Since my daughter Lyla was born, my efforts to reduce the level of toxins in our home have been more than justified. How could I live with myself knowing that I had unnecessarily exposed her to a toxic space? Furthermore, it is good to know that the home she lives in now has gone as far as possible in reducing any negative impact on the environment that will one day be her responsibility. Having a child has really put all these messages into a very clear perspective for me.

In 2005, with my business partner Nikki Blustin, I set up EcoCentric – an online store for well-designed, environmentally conscious homewares. Excited by the diverse culture of sustainability springing up, I wanted to make these products available to a wider design-conscious audience who were turned off by unattractive, functional eco products. EcoCentric has given me a real understanding of the issues surrounding homewares and the impact these seemingly innocuous products have both in the home and upon the environment.

My philosophy of urban eco chic is in some way a reaction to the cheap throwaway consumer society in which we currently find ourselves, where homes appear devoid of authenticity and quality. Too many of the homes I visit are filled with anonymous, low-quality flatpack furniture, where personal expression is traded in for quick, cheap fixes of accessible furniture and nightmarish shopping experiences. Instead, what we need is good, durable design that is multi-functional, easily repaired and manufactured responsibly. I truly believe that we all need to rethink the fundamental criteria of what we term 'contemporary design'. After all, if current design practice does not take into account one of society's major issues, what relevance does it really have to the contemporary needs of our homes, lives and planet?

In an era of eco guilt, worries over debt, fears of terrorism and high levels of work stress, there is a need to create feel-good homes – a space that is as good to live in as it is for the environment. It is far more relaxing to sit back at the end of the day in the knowledge that your home is doing its bit (and saving you money, too). Our homes are a model for the way in which we treat the planet: they are the universe in microcosm. In its truest sense, eco design is about living with as small an environmental footprint as possible – living in smaller homes, using fewer products and resources – a minimalist way of living. However, this is not always possible and so I want to help you find a realistic way to embrace the benefits of eco design through urban eco chic.

For most of us, living in a new, purpose-built eco house will remain an unachievable dream as 98% of the housing stock in the UK is existing period property – and much of it is creaky, leaky and draughty. But do not let that deter you from going eco, as there is so much you can do to make where you already live better, be it a studio, flat, terrace or detached house. After all, you will be adapting what is already existing and so will neither have to produce nor demolish anything. You are just going to make it better and better; now that is a positive thing to do.

I have written this book not with specific examples or brands given but with key information and general suggestions to be investigated further, ideally locally or via the internet. I believe that the eco movement is the most significant development of recent times; it is something we must embrace and work with, seizing the opportunities that it offers. I hope this book opens you up to some of the amazing possibilities that face our homes, and lives, both now and in the future.

ABOVE An elegant expression of urban eco chic. The light-reflective white walls and floors of this beautifully proportioned living room provide the perfect backdrop for a collection of vintage furniture, including a reupholstered sofa in colourful patchwork as well as a mid-twentieth-century Italian standard lamp.

PRINCIPLES

WHY ECO?

IT WAS ARCHITECT
ELIEL SAARINEN WHO SAID,
IN 1956, 'ALWAYS DESIGN A
THING BY CONSIDERING IT IN
ITS NEXT LARGER CONTEXT –
A CHAIR IN A ROOM, A ROOM
IN A HOUSE, A HOUSE IN AN
ENVIRONMENT, AN
ENVIRONMENT IN A
CITY PLAN.'

ABOVE This spacious open-plan kitchen and dining area incorporates a bank of sleek pale plywood units with integral appliances. However, the space is saved from appearing sterile by the addition of a gently worn farmhouse table and assortment of vintage metal chairs, crowned by a glamorous ornate chandelier.

Now, more than ever before, this maxim is applicable to our age – when we must consider everything we design, buy and use in our homes in a wider context. Although this quote predates the current era of eco consciousness, the concept rings truer now than it did in the 1950s – it puts our homes into the context of their surrounding communities and reminds us that small changes in how we live really can make a big difference.

From a technological point of view, our homes are now under ever-closer scrutiny to use less energy, to output less waste and so to become more efficient in their use of the world's resources. That is not surprising when we consider that the average home produces six tonnes of carbon dioxide (CO_2) emissions every year. The CO_2 produced by each home is a 'greenhouse gas', which contributes to global warming and so directly accelerates climate change. If some simple principles were applied to tackling the amount of domestic CO_2 emissions, that figure could easily be reduced by one-third – yes, that is a whole two tonnes less per household. Not only will this lessen the impact that each home has on the environment, it will also save us all money into the bargain.

So if both the message and the motive are clear, why are we not all doing more? There is a misconception that we can live in a more environmentally sustainable way only if we abandon our existing homes to move into shiny new grass-roofed, turbine-powered eco houses; that our old energy-inefficient homes are as leaky as sieves, so why bother improving them?

Well, the reality is that living in a more sustainable way need not entail moving, but you may well need to spend a little money on doing a little maintenance work in order to make your home fit for the twenty-first century. This century looks set to show us that if the existing unsustainable levels of domestic CO_2 emissions continue, it is our own habitable environment we are in danger of destroying, rather than the planet itself. But the problem is, where to start?

WHAT IS ECO DESIGN?

Traditionally, good design for the home has been about bringing together a number of different aspects to create the ideal living space; location, function, style and cost all have to be balanced (with a touch of inspiration, of course) within the perfect home. However, a new and pressing issue has landed upon our doorsteps adding another aspect to designing a home, one that urgently must be considered alongside the rest. Current environmental concerns dictate that our homes must go beyond our personal comfort to become more conscious of the wider needs of the planet. We must consider the impact our homes are having on the environment and how we can all lessen the detrimental effect our choices in life are wreaking on the planet.

In the past, eco design was considered to be the preserve of people generally considered to be tree-hugging hippies, but their ideas are now acknowledged as becoming ever more relevant within today's society. The eco-hippy approach to design could be summed up as 'less is more' – a philosophy that encouraged followers to tread lightly upon the earth.

Some sectors of society were quick to ridicule this ideal – a functional, bare aesthetic intertwined with an alternative spiritual belief system – largely as it presented a rejection of the conventional notions of Western consumerism. But spiritual values aside, from a practical perspective there are many lessons that we can learn from this 'alternative' way of living.

REDUCE, REUSE, RECYCLE

Eco design's fundamental lifestyle 'mantra' (okay, I know that word does sound a little hippy-ish, but stick with it) is known as the 3Rs, that is: **REDUCE** ● **REUSE** ● **RECYCLE**

REDUCE is about reducing your consumption of resources – whether it be the basic utilities that feed your home, such as gas, water and electricity, or more general consumable goods, such as furniture, clothing, packaging and foodstuffs. Being realistic, it does not mean living a frugal, minimalist life but, rather, a more efficient and thoughtful one.

REUSE refers to the sustainable methods by which the products we consume are made. They should come from well-managed sources that are naturally replenished. This includes materials such as wood, wool, cork and rubber. Reuse can also refer to products that have been re-appropriated; this can be as simple as a chair given a new lease on life with a lick of paint or an armchair revived by new upholstery. In addition, it includes other items, from fabrics to foods, that hail from a fairtrade and/or organic source; products that in the process of their manufacture have not unnecessarily depleted or damaged the earth's resources or put others' lives in misery, starvation or poverty.

RECYCLE differs from reuse in that it refers to materials that are totally broken down – used cardboard, glass and paper – before being reassembled in another form to create new products. Recycling ensures that materials are not taken out of their useful lifecycle loop only to be cast into landfill or incinerated. Our planet does not possess limitless supplies of raw materials, so it is essential that we make the most of what we have. It is now possible to recycle nearly 70% of what goes into our homes – glass, tin, paper, plastics, clothes and fabrics, paints – in fact, almost everything can go somewhere if you simply take the time to think about it.

The 3Rs sit in a logical hierarchy. Foremost it is better to consume less. So, in the first instance, **REDUCE** – be efficient with what you use and do not take anything for granted. If you really cannot use less then ensure that what you do consume comes from a well-managed, renewable and sustainable source – in other words **REUSE**. Lastly, make certain that what you do consume does not end up in landfill or incinerated. Prolong the active lifecycle of materials by allowing them to be reused in another form – so **RECYCLE**. Recycling is at the bottom of the 3Rs eco hierarchy because it takes energy to collect materials, chop them up and then re-form them into new products. Nevertheless, recycling plays a vital role in achieving a sustainable world and lifestyle.

> IT IS BETTER TO CONSUME LESS. SO, IN THE FIRST INSTANCE, REDUCE – BE EFFICIENT WITH WHAT YOU USE AND DO NOT TAKE ANYTHING FOR GRANTED.

OPPOSITE This pared-down dining room has a relaxed, unfussy feel. The light-coloured walls keep it fresh and airy – reducing the need for additional artificial light. The use of natural materials, including the timber plank tabletop, offers a simplicity and earthiness whilst the mis-matched vintage chairs add character and stop the space from feeling too precious.

A well-designed eco home incorporates key features based around the 3Rs mantra. The emphasis within any eco home is to reduce the amount of resources it consumes by making the most of the site that it sits on and incorporating the following features within the build:

● Glazing on the building's south side to take in warmth from the sun.
● Minimal openings on the building's north side to reduce heat loss.
● Brise soleil (sun shading louvers) to reduce the amount of summer sun entering the building but to allow the lower winter sun in.
● Renewable energy sources, such as solar water heating, photovoltaic panels or a wind turbine secured to the walls or roof.
● Heavily insulated roofs, walls and ground floors.
● A solid section made from brick, concrete or stone that acts as a heat sink to store the sun's energy (known as thermal mass).
● Double or triple glazed windows.
● An extremely efficient heating system.
● A minimal number of low-energy electrical light fittings.
● A-rated energy-saving appliances, such as fridges and freezers.
● Reduced flow water systems, such as low-flow taps and showers, dual-flush toilets and grey water storage systems.

An eco home can be constructed with sustainable materials including:
🍂 A timber construction with external cladding and fittings, such as doors, window frames and banisters.
🍂 Sheep's wool insulation.
🍂 Natural flooring materials, such as wood, wool or cork.
🍂 Non-toxic natural paints.
🍂 A green turfed roof that insulates and encourages local biodiversity.

Lastly, an efficient eco home will consider what resources can be recycled and make the most of them in the following ways:
● Grey (used) water recycling system.
● Heat recovery systems to recycle surplus warm air.
❋ Recyclable materials, such as stainless steel and wood surfaces.
🍂 Recycling bins in the kitchen and a compost heap in the garden.

ECO DESIGN VERSUS ECO CHIC

While the 3Rs mantra, which lies at the very heart of eco design, appears rather basic, this apparent simplicity belies its complex nature when applied in its strictest form. Within the creation of an environmentally friendly home, staying true to core eco design principles presents some fascinating challenges. An eco house is a utilitarian piece of design in which functional efficiency is placed above all else; any nod towards style is considered a bonus. After all, in the face of such an enormous issue as global warming and the destruction of our habitat, why would we consider trivialities such as style to be important?

The creation of eco-efficient homes is a noble aim for architects and designers to strive towards. The world of design is courageously doing battle with the wastefulness of society; but – and this is a big but – there is a fundamental problem with architectural efficiency and the nature of human beings. We are emotional creatures; we have passions, likes, dislikes and, just occasionally, we are a little irrational. We are guided by our instincts and act upon emotional responses. For many the spare minimalism that accompanies the ultra efficiency of pure eco design can be a real turnoff; our personal needs are often more complex than its minimal specifications allow.

Eco design has provided the architectural theory and technological know-how by which to design the energy-efficient House of the Future, but I question whether it will help you to create the perfect Home of the Future. When creating a home, I want colour, atmosphere, personality and soul – and I, for one, am not prepared to give these things up readily.

Here I see a dichotomy between the asceticism eco purists dictate we need to live by in order to be green and the emotionalism inherent in all of us that fuels our personal desire for comfort. Acting as a bridge between the extreme eco minimalism espoused by activists and the universal human need to create a nurturing space, eco chic offers up a sustainable way of living that is at once comfortable and enticing. Eco chic is a decorating style that follows the concepts of eco design yet does not expect you to forgo the level of style that we have all come to demand within our homes.

ECO CHIC OFFERS UP A SUSTAINABLE WAY OF LIVING THAT IS AT THE SAME TIME COMFORTABLE AND ENTICING.

Sustainable living is all about community; after all, what is the point in only one house within a city being environmentally conscious. A community offers us all the opportunity to work together, to share resources and to make financial savings. If eco design in its purest form does not excite and inspire the masses, it will be taken up by only a minority. With ambitious quotas in the reduction of carbon emissions being set, such limited appeal is a huge problem. Eco chic, however, allows us to create energy efficient homes that are beautifully designed, and really stimulate and excite us by appealing to our emotional sides.

URBAN ECO CHIC

The society we live in is a highly visual one, with style messages constantly being played out on the television and within the media. As a result, style plays a key role in our personal expression – it is an essential outlet for the way that we present ourselves to the world – announcing what we like and dislike, our experiences, our preferences and our social grouping. A world without style is practically unimaginable. Can you envisage a world where you lived in a sterile white box and dressed in the same way every day – and, worse still, where everyone around you did the same?

Although the dilemma of deciding what to wear each day would be a thing of the past, there would be no self-expression or individuality. Instead, it would be a soulless and anonymous existence. Clearly, design has a key role to play in so many aspects of our lives that we cannot be expected to just drop it when designing our homes. I believe that good design can actually help us to embrace essential trends, and in that way make the pure functionality of eco design a sweeter, more aspirational choice. Okay, so it may be a little more challenging to go green, but that is exactly why we have to exercise a little creativity in this problem solving.

In my emotionally led designer's mind, style always comes first. Good design seduces you; it compels you to respond emotionally; in short, it will make you fall in love with a product or a space. Tapping into this emotional response is essential if a movement such as eco design is to be embraced universally.

Urban eco chic is about creating a balance between style and function, with a conscious effort to reduce one's environmental impact. It is a thoughtful style that considers the wider impact of design on the environment in which it exists. It is now impossible to discuss modern design without sustainability being a key part of that debate. Good design must be beautiful, functional, and now inherently green.

The performance of each product we use is now critical. It is a subject that we are all familiar with when discussing cars: we would not contemplate buying a car without first asking how many miles to the gallon it does, how fast it is 0 to 60 mph, or how many seats it has. But only now are we starting to realise that performance (as boring a concept as it may seem) also relates to our homes. Performance is not solely about energy efficiency; it is also about the use of space, storage and multi-functional adaptability.

Urban eco chic brings together the demands of performance with the style-led aspects of contemporary living. It is a pioneering style, one for a new age of social and environmental development, a style to embrace as a community – one that benefits us all and generations to come. When you start to see the bigger picture of what a style movement can really do, it becomes even more exciting.

OPPOSITE This bedroom uses recycled floorboards to stunning effect on a feature wall, bringing texture to the space and creating a wonderful visual contrast with the luxurious curtains. Organic fairtrade bedlinen encourages a sound night's sleep in a toxin-free environment, enhanced by the knowledge that it is ethically produced. Hardwood flooring, teamed with just a small bedside rug, helps to keep the space dust- and allergen-free.

KEY ECO QUESTIONS TO ASK OF EVERY MATERIAL AND PRODUCT

Where has it come from?

● Is it from a naturally renewable source?

● Was it made in a non-polluting, energy efficient manner?

● Were the rights of the workers respected with good conditions, reasonable hours and fair pay?

● Will it travel vast distances to reach me? Can I choose a locally made product instead?

How will I use it?

● Will it be energy efficient, saving me money and saving the environment carbon emissions?

● Is it built to last, or will it fall apart as soon as the guarantee ends?

● Is it easy to maintain and fix? Am I able to get spare parts easily?

Where will it go once I am done with it?

● Can I pass it on to someone else to use after I have finished with it?

● Can I recycle it easily?

● Will it biodegrade?

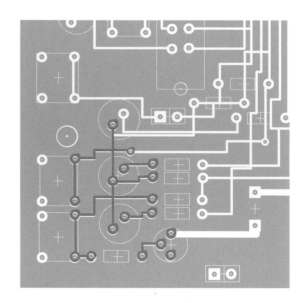

ASPECTS OF URBAN ECO CHIC

THE THREE ESSENTIAL ASPECTS OF URBAN ECO CHIC WILL HELP YOU TO BOTH FUNCTIONALLY REDUCE YOUR ENVIRONMENTAL IMPACT, AS WELL AS CREATE AN AESTHETIC STYLE THAT REFLECTS THESE IDEAS AND EXPRESSES YOUR PERSONALITY.

TECHNOLOGY

Technology is the key to how we can reduce our environmental impact and lower our carbon emissions. It is an exciting area, which is constantly developing. Modern technology is becoming smaller, better, faster and, most importantly, more efficient. Embracing all that technology has to offer will allow us to make our lives less wasteful and more efficient and to harness more of what occurs naturally around us – such as renewable energies from the sun, wind, earth and sea, helping us to reduce our impact on the environment and to combat climate change. Technology refers to methods of creating renewable energy, super-insulating materials and ultra-efficient appliances, but also to cutting-edge materials, be they new low-impact materials, natural or even recycled. They often have a clean sleek look that sets up a perfect textural contrast to offset the beauties of natural and vintage materials and objects.

NATURE

Nature is an essential component of our lives that we sometimes take for granted. Interaction with nature is a grounding force; it quite literally brings us back down to earth and reminds us we are part of the natural world. The vibrant scent of freshly mown grass, the textural feel of tree bark, the flickering flames of a log fire – these all raise simple but primeval emotional responses within us, which are essentially comforting. Natural materials often improve with age and use, developing a unique character, adding individuality and a certain richness to any home.

The use of natural materials not only brings textural sensuality to the home, but also allows us to choose sustainable and naturally renewable materials – materials that, when responsibly managed, have a lower impact on the environment. If chosen and finished carefully, nature will allow you to reduce the number of man-made toxins in your home, creating a healthier space to live in.

VINTAGE

'Vintage' is an umbrella term that opens us up to the grandeur of antiques, ingenuity of reused objects and excitement of flea-market finds. It is about making the most of what we have already produced (and so requires no new objects to be made) and inventing new ways to use them – offering a new lease on life for an item that someone else has discarded. The pleasure of vintage is all about invention – putting a new spin on an existing object – be that through repositioning, framing, grouping or remaking.

Beyond finding ways to reuse items, it is about harnessing the style inherent within vintage objects, reflecting our experiences, personalities and cultural identities and creating individual spaces that reflect a little of who we are. Vintage items have a softening effect; wear and tear simply cannot be reproduced, so vintage pieces take the harder edges off a contemporary interior. In this age of mass production, we yearn for individual objects that possess character – aspects that in some way rub off onto us, revealing our own identities and curiosities.

The three aspects of urban eco chic can be interpreted in a number of ways and can help solve style and functional dilemmas when trying to create your own eco home. What we will discover is that certain rooms of the home naturally show a bias towards one of these three aspects over the other two, due to their function and status as a public/private space or as one that uses more or fewer resources.

⦿ Kitchens have a heavier slant towards technology, as this is an area where many resources (gas, water, electricity) are used and so need to be as efficient as possible.

🍂 Kitchens may also lean towards nature for some materials, which may align with our tastes for natural and organic foods.

🍂 Bathrooms may have a heavier slant to nature, as this is a sensual space, so using natural materials to create a spa-like feel will be very relaxing, while technology will help us to reduce our use of resources.

❀ Bedrooms, being private spaces, may have a greater leaning towards the vintage, which carries romantic, nostalgic associations, while nature will lend a sense of simplicity and purity.

🍂 ❀ ⦿ Living rooms may well lean towards nature, vintage and then technology, being public spaces – thus reflecting a variety of your interests and activities, such as books, music, ornaments, photographs, music or film.

In this way urban eco chic is open to a certain amount of personal interpretation; it is a flexible style through which you can express your own tastes and experiences while sustaining your passions for a cleaner, greener way of living.

ABOVE This living room favours the nature and vintage aspects of urban eco chic, to create a relaxed yet personal space that speaks volumes about the owners. Sometimes

the technological elements of a room can be hidden;
underfloor heating beneath the reclaimed boards, keeps
this space cosy with no visible heat source.

RESOURCES

ECO CONSCIENCE

IT IS IMPORTANT TO REMEMBER THAT URBAN ECO CHIC IS A STYLE WITH A CONSCIENCE. IT IS MORE THAN JUST THIS SEASON'S COLOUR; IT IS, RATHER, A WAY OF LIFE. UNUSUALLY, IT IS ONE THAT BALANCES STYLISTIC CHOICES WITH TECHNICAL PERFORMANCE TO PRODUCE INTERIORS THAT ARE BOTH STYLISH AND SUSTAINABLE.

It is important to consider the bigger picture of the ways in which we live and to get out of the short-term view that saving small amounts of money now is our primary objective. I feel it is better to consider the possible greater long-term gains and to take a level of social responsibility for our actions.

Like many parents, I was compelled by the birth of my daughter to think hard about our environmental future and whether I was personally doing as much as I could towards securing a safe habitat for our future generations. If we do not take action against climate change now, our own children will face an even greater threat. Much of the campaigning around environmental issues is designed to tug on our guilty heartstrings. But although our foe – the notorious carbon emissions – is invisible, it is clear we all must act fast.

For a long time, guilt has been a key ally in the battle to convert people to a more sustainable mode of living, but I believe it need not be that way. There is a direct necessity for a change in attitude towards adopting eco-friendly measures within our homes, but we could be doing it through positive free will and

OPPOSITE With urban eco chic there is no compromise when it comes to style – it is about creating a home that is as good to live with as it is for the environment. In my own home, form, function and environmental thinking work together to create a space that is equally as luxurious as it is healthy.

aspiration, rather than through negative guilt. Even something as seemingly mundane as an eco-efficient home can be an exciting challenge if looked upon with vision – not to mention the fact that with energy prices on the rise, our homes are becoming ever more expensive to run. So the possible saving in fuel costs could be a clear incentive to take action.

We could be actively embracing change. After all, there are so many positive benefits to be had – not least, the amount of money to be saved. More than that, there is the legacy we will leave behind for our children and grandchildren through reducing the impact that our homes are needlessly having on the environment.

WHAT IS A CARBON FOOTPRINT?

You cannot fail to have noticed all the recent talk of carbon. Just a few years ago, the only carbon we all worried about was the stuff we scraped off our burnt toast! However, the word 'carbon' has crept up on us and is now one of society's burning issues (if you will excuse the pun).

When discussing a carbon footprint, what we are really referring to is carbon dioxide (CO_2) emissions. In a nutshell, CO_2 is produced every time we make or burn something, and so virtually every action we take contributes to our carbon footprint. The real problem occurs when we excavate fossil fuels – coal, oil and gas – which for millions of years have been buried under the earth, and introduce them into our living environment. When these resources are burned they produce energy, some of which we use, some of which is lost and some of which becomes CO_2.

CO_2 is one of the 'greenhouse gases' and, much as their name suggests, these gases have a warming effect on our environment. Energy from the sun is mainly absorbed by the earth's surface, but around 30% of this energy is reflected back into the atmosphere in infrared wavelengths. The increasing presence of CO_2 and other greenhouse gases in the earth's atmosphere since industrialisation has resulted in more of this infrared energy being trapped within the earth's lower atmosphere, rather than escaping into space. Once trapped, it causes a further warming of the atmosphere, known as the 'greenhouse effect'. This process has led to global warming, wreaking all sorts of damage upon the balance of our environment.

The problem with CO_2 is that the damn stuff is invisible. So just how do we start to take with due seriousness something we cannot physically see ? And concerning ourselves with our own carbon footprint is all very well, but why should we be individually responsible if it is really heavy industry and distant power stations that are churning out all this CO_2?

The truth is that almost every action we take – however trivial – has an impact on the environment; even the simple act of switching on a light sends a message to the power station to burn more fuel and produce more CO_2. If we add up the CO_2 emissions associated with all those individual actions, it produces what is termed a carbon footprint. Simply put, a carbon footprint is a measure in units (or tonnes) of CO_2 of how your life's activities impact on the environment in terms of the greenhouse gases produced.

There are two aspects to your carbon footprint:
• A primary footprint is produced as a direct result of your day-to-day activities, such as your use of gas, electricity and water in the home and through car journeys.
• A secondary footprint is created through the indirect choices that you make and reflect the CO_2 produced by the whole lifecycle of the products you choose. For example, you buy a plastic hairdryer made in China, which travels around the globe, uses lots of energy before it eventually dies, is then thrown away and ends up in a landfill site where it slowly decomposes over the following 200,000 years or so. Phew! This single purchase will undoubtedly have a high carbon footprint, so it is critical that you examine the lifecycle of each product that you consume and consider its environmental impact.

Share of public services 12%

Financial services 3%

Recreation and leisure 14%

Household (buildings and furnishings) 9%

Car manufacture 7%

Clothes and personal effects 4%

Food and drink 5%

Holiday flights 6%

Public transport 3%

Private transport 10%

Electricity 12%

Gas, oil and coal 15%

A TYPICAL CARBON FOOTPRINT

The chart above gives a basic breakdown of an average person's carbon footprint in the UK, highlighting the areas in which we create the most damage to the environment. It shows just how much work we have really got to do in the areas of our homes, recreation and leisure, and transport. That narrows it down then!

The efficiency of our homes is becoming ever more important. Gone are the energy-rich years of the last century. We can no longer afford to be wasteful when it comes to the amount of gas and electricity we consume. Now we are living in an age when what we use and what we produce are being scrutinised –

and with good reason. Our homes are estimated to create nearly one-third of all the CO_2 greenhouse gases produced in the UK – that is nearly six tonnes of CO_2 per household per year. If action were taken, with just a few simple measures, that figure could be reduced by one-third. In this way, your home reduces its impact on the environment, you create a healthier and more comfortable space to live in and, of course, you spend less money.

When it is put like this, why wouldn't we all want to make the switch to a cleaner, greener way of living? After all, why should our homes impact unnecessarily on the environment when they really do not have to?

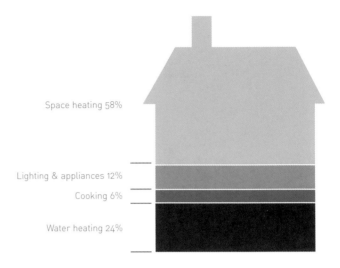

Space heating 58%

Lighting & appliances 12%

Cooking 6%

Water heating 24%

HOME RESOURCES

AN ECO EFFICIENT HOME MINIMISES ITS USE OF RESOURCES – THAT IS GAS, ELECTRICITY AND WATER. IT IS IMPORTANT TO UNDERSTAND HOW A HOME FUNCTIONS IN ORDER TO IDENTIFY WHERE THE MOST EFFECTIVE CHANGES CAN BE MADE TO REDUCE RESOURCES USAGE. WITH CAREFUL PLANNING, THIS STRICT CODE OF REDUCTION NEED NOT LEAD TO A COMPROMISED LIFESTYLE.

AVERAGE ENERGY USE IN THE HOME

This chart shows the proportional domestic energy use within the average home. It clearly demonstrates how important the heating of your home and water are to your overall energy consumption (and your carbon footprint). If you are going to focus your energies into doing your bit, your time and money are best spent insulating the roof, walls and floor of your home; sealing up draughts; insulating pipes and water tanks, fitting energy efficient boilers and white goods (fridges, freezers and washing machines) and kitting your home out with low-energy lightbulbs.

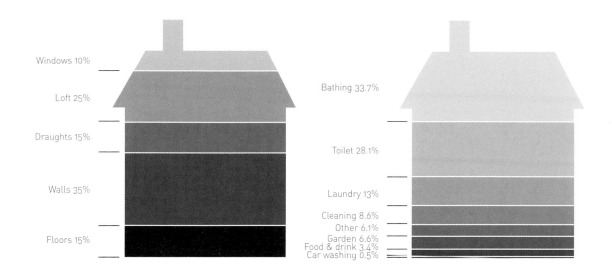

Windows 10%
Loft 25%
Draughts 15%
Walls 35%
Floors 15%

Bathing 33.7%
Toilet 28.1%
Laundry 13%
Cleaning 8.6%
Other 6.1%
Garden 6.6%
Food & drink 3.4%
Car washing 0.5%

AVERAGE HEAT LOSS IN THE HOME

The statistics shown in this chart prove that, surprisingly, more heat escapes through your walls than it does through your roof. So if you are going to spend any money, install cavity wall as well as loft insulation. If you are going for a bigger refurbishment consider it's well worth fitting energy efficient double glazing and insulating under the floors as well. Check with your local authority to see if you can get a grant to assist, it all helps. However, do not forget the simple things; if you can feel a draught, track down the source and fix it – the warm, heated air within your home is being cooled down by the chilly air rushing in. These measures will not only help to cut your carbon footprint and save you money, but will also, most importantly, help to make your home cosy and warm to live in.

AVERAGE WATER USE IN THE HOME

Amazingly, the water we drink and cook with accounts for only a tiny percentage of what we use on average at home. If you are serious about cutting your water usage – and bills – you should be washing with less water (for example, taking showers rather than baths – or shorter showers, if you tend to linger in them). Remember that you pay for hot water 3 times; once to buy it, again to heat it and finally for it to be taken away again. You will also need to do something about that wasteful toilet. Almost a third of your entire water usage is flushed away (and that's drinking water that you are flushing, so please don't waste it). It is a little-known fact that water supplies and sewerage account for 3% of the UK's energy use, so it is not just about the amount of water you use; it is also about the energy it takes to get it to and from your home.

LIFESTYLE CHANGES
LOW COST

SO HOW DO YOU START CUTTING BACK ON THE AMOUNT OF RESOURCES YOU USE AT HOME? THESE SIMPLE TIPS ARE GREAT FOR THOSE WHO DON'T HAVE THE CASH TO SPLASH. IN FACT, UNLIKE SOME GREEN MEASURES, WHICH ENTAIL EXTRA SPENDING, MANY OF THESE TIPS WILL ACTUALLY SAVE YOU MONEY.

ELECTRICITY

● Switch to a green energy supplier who provides power from renewable sources.

● Do not leave appliances on standby; turn them off at the plug as they use power even when on standby.

● Turn off the lights as you leave each room.

● Keep windows clean, so they let in lots of natural light; you will use less electric lighting.

● Position white or reflective surfaces, such as white tables and mirrors, near windows to bounce light around – it is amazingly effective. Painting walls white also helps.

● When boiling water for drinks, fill the kettle with only as much water as you need.

● Open fridge and freezer doors for as short a time as possible to prevent cool air from escaping. Keep them fully stocked, as the mass stores the coolness longer.

● Use a good-quality washing powder and wash at a low temperature such as 30°C; over a year it saves an amazing amount of energy.

● Air dry your washing outside to cut out the use of a tumble drier.

● Cook with the lids on saucepans.

● Turn the lights off for an hour or two each evening and dine in romantic candlelight.

● Close blinds or curtains during the summer so the sun's warmth does not overheat your home.

GAS

🔴 Turn down the thermostat controlling your heating by 1°C – it will cut your heating bill by up to 10%. You are unlikely to notice the difference.

🔴 Programme the timer controlling your heating to go off 30 minutes before you leave the house and back on again just before you return home.

🔴 Turn down the temperature on your boiler to 60°C, so hot water is usable straight from the tap and does not need to be mixed with cold.

🔴 Fit temporary double glazing – a plastic sheet adhered to the inner frame of a window, tightened with the use of a hairdryer. It makes a massive difference and yet is cheap to do.

🔴 Thick blinds or curtains insulate the windows and prevent heat loss; look for vintage ones at second-hand shops, markets or online.

🔴 In the cooler months, open all blinds and curtains to allow the building's mass to soak up any heat from the sun.

🔴 A shelf positioned over a radiator helps to kick the heat forward and stops it circulating up to the ceiling.

🔴 Fit silver foil-covered boards (make or buy them) behind your radiators; they are amazingly effective at directing heat into the room.

🔴 Fit simple draught excluders, such as thick curtains, over doors and block up any disused fireplaces to cut draughts.

WATER

🔴 Get a water meter fitted, then you will be directly responsible only for the water you use.

🔴 Turn down the valves fitted within the pipes below the taps. But be careful not to turn them down too much otherwise the flow will not be great enough to fire up your boiler for hot water.

🔴 Take a shower instead of a bath; this can use just two-fifths of the 100 litres a bath uses. A word of caution, though: a power shower can use more than a bath in just five minutes.

🔴 If you are going to take a bath, share it.

🔴 Do not leave the tap running whilst you are brushing your teeth.

🔴 Avoid unnecessary flushes of your toilet. Each flush may use up to nine litres of water.

🔴 Fit a cistern displacement device (CDD) to save three litres of water with every flush.

🔴 Fix any dripping taps.

🔴 Wait until you have a full load before using your washing machine or dishwasher. Alternatively, use an economy or half-load programme. Modern A-rated appliances are more efficient than cleaning by hand.

🔴 Keep a jug of water cool in the fridge, instead of running the tap until it goes cold.

🔴 If you use a garden hose, fit a trigger nozzle so no water is wasted.

🔴 Instead of a hosepipe, use a bucket and sponge to wash the car the old-fashioned way.

LIFESTYLE CHANGES
MEDIUM COST

THESE ARE THE TIPS TO SAVE YOU MORE MONEY OVER A LONGER TERM. OKAY, THEY WILL COST A LITTLE CASH TO IMPLEMENT BUT IN TIME YOU WILL REAP MUCH GREATER REWARDS THAN THE INITIAL LAYOUT. YOU MAY WANT TO CONSIDER THESE IF YOU ARE REFURBISHING YOUR HOME, DOING SOME DIY OR MOVING INTO A NEW PLACE.

ELECTRICITY

● Fit low-energy lightbulbs – when you move, you can always take them with you (although that could be considered a bit mean). An energy-saving bulb can use one sixth of the electricity and last twelve times as long as a conventional bulb. The yearly savings far outweigh the extra cost of the bulb.

● Fit an infrared sensor switch to turn on and off the lights, such as exterior security lights (these devices do not work with low-energy bulbs), that are used infrequently. No more fumbling for light switches in the dark.

● Buy a portable energy meter. This brilliant gadget has two parts: the first part connects to your electricity meter and sends a signal to the second part, which can be carried around the home. The latter tells you how much electricity is being used at any one moment, alerting you to lights, stereos and any other appliances left on. It can save you up to 25% of your electricity bill.

● Purchase A-rated appliances, such as fridges, freezers and washing machines, with an energy-saving certificate. Remember, once they leave the showroom they will cost you less money to run on a daily basis, and the chances are they will last longer too.

● Use 'everything off' switches that prevent technology such as DVD players and TVs from being left on standby and wasting energy.

GAS

◉ Get your boiler serviced annually; it will run more efficiently.

◉ Fit a thermostatic radiator valve (TRV) to each of your radiators; they allow better control of the temperature within each room as they respond to the temperate in that room rather than relying on a single thermostat in a draughty hallway to control the temperature of your entire home.

◉ Encase your hot water storage tank in an insulating jacket; this can save around 75% of the average heat lost. If the outside of the tank feels warm, you must insulate it. Remember to insulate the hot water pipes, too.

◉ Seal up draughts. Amazingly, draughts account for 15% of the heat loss from a typical home. Fit draught excluders wherever you have a door or window opening. Consider fitting foam or copper strips to doorways, brushes to windows and rotating flaps to cover keyholes. Wherever you can feel cold air coming in, warm air is escaping. It is as simple as that.

◉ Fit either proprietary or secondary double glazing to insulate your home and reduce noise levels. Otherwise a simple acrylic sheet placed over your existing windows will be cheaper than a whole new double glazing system, it will make your home both warmer and quieter.

WATER

◉ Upgrade your toilet to a water efficient model by retro-fitting it with a dual flush kit attached to the syphon. These only release water into the pan when the handle is depressed, and do not release the whole cistern of water. This can reduce toilet water usage from 42 litres per day to 21 litres – 50% less! Kits can be bought online, and do work well.

◉ Fit an external water butt that connects directly to your roof gutters. Roofs catch and drain tens of thousands of litres of rainwater each year – this could fill hundreds of water butts with free water which would be perfect for watering the garden or washing the car.

◉ Fit an aerated eco shower head, which simply screws onto your old shower hose. It will save an incredible 75% of the water you use in your shower without you even noticing it. It replaces water with air bubbles, creating an effervescent flow which was a wonderful feeling on the skin, with no apparent reduction in water use.

LIFESTYLE CHANGES
HIGH COST

THESE TIPS ARE FOR THE SERIOUSLY COMMITTED AND THOSE AIMING TOWARDS A TOTAL ECO REFURBISHMENT. I HAVE KEPT THEM SHORT, FOR THE TECHNOLOGY IN MANY OF THESE AREAS IS DEVELOPING FAST AND SO EACH PURCHASING DECISION SHOULD BE THOROUGHLY RESEARCHED BEFORE PROCEEDING – THE INTERNET OR A TRADE SHOW IS A GOOD PLACE TO START.

ELECTRICITY

● Fit external shutters to your windows; they will reduce any heat gain from the sun to keep rooms cooler during summer and cut back any heat loss in winter.

● Cut down on the need for tumble drying by building a covered area or lean-to for airing washing naturally.

● Install a new lighting system throughout your home, using a mixture of low-energy bulbs, light emitting diodes (LEDs) and compact fluorescent tubes.

● Look into generating your own electricity. Fit either photovoltaic panels or a wind turbine – but only if you live somewhere very exposed and windy – to your roof. (See the section on renewable energies, pages 38–43.)

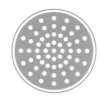

GAS

◉ If your boiler is over 15 years old it is probably inefficient. Fit a modern condensing combination boiler, which may be over 90% efficient.

◉ Insulate your attic (see page 81 for a description of organic sheep's wool, the best eco insulating product). Use at least 27cm of insulation to prevent heat loss.

◉ Insulate your walls with external, internal or cavity wall insulation. It is imperative you tackle this as 35% of all heat loss occurs through walls.

◉ Insulate your floors. This can be done to suspended floors – but take care not to block any natural ventilation – and solid concrete floors, which draw heat away from a room.

◉ Fit underfloor heating using an energy-saving water-heating system. It creates a comfortable environment in which heat rises evenly. By eliminating unsightly radiators, it facilitates furnishing your home; and it reduces the need for wall-to-wall carpeting, with its allergy-affecting dust build-up.

◉ Double or triple glaze your windows. Low e-argon filled panels are most efficient. Choose wood frames, which are less damaging than aluminium or Upvc. Timber frames last as long as the other options when properly maintained.

◉ Fit solar water-heating tubes to your roof to provide hot water for your bathrooms and kitchen (see page 41 for more on this).

WATER

◉ Move your boiler closer to the area where you use the most hot water to reduce what is known as the 'dead leg'. This means you do not have to run the taps for such a long time before the water flows hot.

◉ Fit low-flow taps to your kitchen and bathroom sinks. These taps aerate the flow of water to give the effect of a greater flow rate, but use less water.

◉ Install an underground water butt that supplies water to feed your washing machine and toilets.

◉ Use a grey water system that will reuse bath and shower water for flushing toilets.

◉ Replace old toilets with super efficient, designed pan and syphon models. These will use just 4 litres on a full flush, compared to a traditional toilet which could use 9 or 12 litres per flush.

◉ Fit dual flow taps with water saving cartridges. The taps' two settings have a water brake between them which prevents the tap from being fully opened straight away.

RENEWABLE ENERGIES

Harnessing the non-polluting energy that occurs naturally around us makes a whole lot of sense. Why pay good money to excavate and burn finite fossil fuels when we can gather power from renewable sources such as the sun, wind and water for free. It sounds obvious, doesn't it? However, in reality it is not that cheap, for the start-up costs for harnessing these forms of energy can be high. Furthermore, we are encouraged to buy our resources from the conventional power suppliers through the convenient pipes and cables they feed into our homes. For those living in towns and cities, it is often not feasible to hook a wind turbine to a roof or balcony.

There is a general misconception that in order to have a truly eco-conscious home you must have a gleaming, shiny (and fast-spinning) wind turbine proudly strapped to your roof. If the truth be known, many of the technologies used to capture these renewable energy sources are yet to be as efficient as their manufacturers (and retailers) claim, and with high purchase and installation costs, the payback periods are long.

In time this will change, but for now it is worth doing your research and speaking to those who have already installed any renewable energy device that may have pricked your eco conscience. On the plus side, many eco-friendly home improvements qualify for assistance grants to pay for a portion of the costs (thereby shortening the payback period), which are worth investigating in parallel. Often retailers are able to help you research these grants.

The general feeling amongst experts is that the wisest investment is in making your home as efficient as possible. Super-insulate all walls, roofs, floors and openings. Make your home airtight by sealing up any draughts around doors, windows and chimneys, while ensuring some degree of natural ventilation in each room. Fit double glazing to insulate all windows and install the most efficient appliances you can afford. Only once you have made your home efficient should you start to think about investing money in renewable energies; otherwise you are simply pouring your money through a leaky sieve. However, it is helpful to know the basics of each system so you can make informed choices.

Of the methods suggested, solar water heating is considered the most viable, giving you up to 50% of your hot water and having the shortest payback period. Next photovoltaics offer a good solution to reducing your electrical needs, and technology is set to make this increasingly efficient. Biomass boilers are likely to become smaller and more domestically friendly in years to come, so it is worth considering them (as well as wood burning stoves) as options for low CO_2 energy. Other solutions such as wind turbines and ground source heat pumps are perhaps best used in a remote area where you may live away from the National Grid and need to produce your own energy or must pay a high price to have it installed – so making the payback period more reasonable.

OPPOSITE Making the most of natural light by keeping windows clean and bouncing light off internal surfaces can help keep your gas and electricity usage down.

PASSIVE SOLAR HEATING

The good news is that, in some small way, your home already soaks up energy from the sun via the materials it is made of; this is known as 'passive solar gains'. What you need to learn is how to manage and maximise its benefits.

Any of the sun's rays that hit the outside or inside of your home create heat. In the summer this can make your home too hot, but, if maximised, in the winter it can help to reduce the amount of energy needed to heat your home. The two most common ways to soak up the heat from the sun are through windows and conservatories. However, the problem is that they are also the means by which a home loses the most heat or becomes overheated. If you follow these basic principles, you can get your home to work a little harder for you and can keep it more comfortable all year round.

TO PREVENT HEAT LOSS AND CAPTURE HEAT FROM THE SUN

● On the south side of your home use dense flooring materials, such as stone or ceramic tiles, which have a higher thermal mass, to soak up and store any heat that comes through your glazing. It is released slowly throughout the day. Pile carpets and wooden floorboards have a lower thermal mass because they are not so dense and so they do not store heat.

● Whenever possible, reduce the windows on the north side of your home to a minimum, and ensure that they are double glazed, whilst still letting in some light, since no direct sunlight will enter your home on this side.

● Cover windows at night with thick curtains, blinds or shutters.

● If you have a conservatory, fit a door between it and the rest of the house, which will help you control heat coming in or going out in the winter.

● Fit additional glazing to your windows; this may be temporary, proprietary or double glazing (of which low e-argon filled units are most efficient).

TO PREVENT OVERHEATING

● Plant a deciduous tree outside your south-facing windows. When its leaves are out in the summer, it will naturally shade your home from the sun; and in the winter it will allow the lower winter sun to shine through its bare branches allowing heat in. Isn't nature clever?

● Fit external shutters to open and close over your windows (as they do around the Mediterranean). When kept closed during the day, the shutters will minimise heat from the sun entering your home and keep it cooler.

● Fit slatted Venetian blinds, which allow you to control the amount of sunlight entering the room, reducing the intense summer sun and allowing in the weaker winter sun.

● If you are planning to add a conservatory to your home, resist the temptation to choose one with a glass roof. Choose a solid roof (or one with roof lights, if you must) that cuts out the excess heat gained from the high summer sun, but allows in the lower winter sun. It will also allow you to insulate the roof, making it a more usable space year round.

● Ventilate your home properly; this can be as simple as opening windows on both sides of your home to allow airflow or even using an extractor fan (but the latter will use energy and cost you money).

SOLAR WATER HEATING

A solar water heating unit – using energy from the sun – works alongside your conventional heating system to provide hot water for use in bathrooms and kitchens. Because hot water is needed all year round, solar water heating is one of the most useful forms of renewable energies as it can be used on overcast days. Over a year, solar water heating can, on average, provide up to 50% of your hot-water needs.

There are various kinds of solar water heating systems, but they can be divided into two basic types: active and passive. Both types include a solar collector and one or more storage tanks. Solar water heating systems are made up of three parts:

SOLAR COLLECTOR – which needs to be positioned on a south-facing angle, ideally at 68° from the horizontal, so usually on a roof. For domestic use, they typically take the form of either a large, rectangular, glass-fronted panel or a series of long glass tubes (called evacuated tubes, because the air has been withdrawn from them), that can be connected together depending on how many are needed.

HEAT TRANSFER SYSTEM – which converts the solar energy collected to heat the water.

WATER STORAGE CYLINDER – which collects the hot water to be used when you wish. This must be well insulated, of course.

Solar water heating is generally considered to be the most efficient way to incorporate renewable energy into your home, particularly as the installation costs can be offset with grants. However, you will still need to fit a conventional water heating system, which will work in parallel, for those times when the solar water heating unit is not producing enough power, for example on rainy, wintry days.

GROUND-SOURCE HEAT PUMPS

Ground-source heat pumps transfer the natural warmth of the earth to your home's heating system. Whereas the air temperature above ground fluctuates, reaching extremes in the winter and summer months, the ground just below the earth's surface remains at a year-round constant of 11–12°C. This energy can be converted into hot water and pumped around a domestic heating system or it can be used to pre-heat water that is then drawn into the hot-water system, making it more efficient.

Ground-source heat pump systems are made up of three parts:

WATER LOOP – which is a closed loop of plastic pipe, filled with water and anti-freeze. This can be buried underground in a shallow horizontal trench, about 1.25–2.5m deep, which must accommodate a 125–185m length of pipe. The ground area required can be reduced by arranging the pipe in overlapping coils. Where ground space is limited a deep vertical well of 50–60m can be used, although this is a more expensive method. With both methods, the fluid is fed along the loop, slowly warms up and then is returned inside the home to the heat pump.

HEAT PUMP – which converts and condenses the low levels of heat from the water loop into usable warm water (much like a fridge working in reverse). This unit consumes electrical energy, which is needed to force the water around the system, so it can make ground-source heat pumps less efficient. However, a heat pump can be combined with a photovoltaic cell to generate the power it needs. This warm water is then fed through your heating system.

HEATING SYSTEM – which can either be in the form of radiators (although they need to be larger than average as the water within the heating system is not so hot) or ideally an underfloor heating system, which uses lower levels of water to more comfortably heat a space.

Whilst ground-source heat-pump systems sound great in theory, they are not as efficient as conventional gas-fired central heating systems. So if you are on mains gas, use that. If you are not and otherwise use electricity or oil to heat your water, a ground-source heat-pump system would massively cut the amount of CO_2 produced by your home.

PHOTOVOLTAICS

Solar PV or photovoltaic panels convert simple daylight – energy from the sun – through layers of silicon into electrical energy, which can then be used in the home. Because they do not actually need to be exposed to the sun, they create energy even on a cloudy day.

Positioned on a roof, in order to pick up the most energy the panels will ideally be oriented towards the path of the sun – in the UK, this is in a southerly direction. The direct current (DC) electricity – similar to that which comes from a battery – produced by the panels can either be sold on to the National Grid via an inverter and an export meter or stored in a battery prior to being altered through an inverter to an alternating current (AC), which can then be used as mains power within your home.

Most photovoltaic panels take the form of surface-mounted units, although some manufacturers are now producing less conspicuous versions in the form of slim grey roof tiles, which look much like natural slate, but these are the more expensive option. If you choose the former, the panels will have a visual impact on your home, so in places such as conservation areas you will need to seek planning permission before fitting them. In addition they can be very heavy, so it is best to make totally sure that your roof can actually support them. Seek the opinion of an engineer or experienced builder.

The great thing about photovoltaic panels is that they produce CO_2-free electricity and are very low in maintenance. However, the main drawbacks are the cost of the panels and their relative effectiveness. In some cases, the payback period may be longer than the estimated 30-year lifespan of the units themselves. This could change if the units become more efficient, electricity becomes more expensive or the panels simply become cheaper to buy. That being said, it is possible to get grants from local authorities to help pay for photovoltaic panels.

HEAT RECOVERY SYSTEM

This takes stale, moist air from certain warm rooms (such as bathrooms and kitchens) filters it, mixes it with fresh air from an exterior source and then redistributes it to other areas of the home. The benefits are two fold – it ventilates the home, preventing the build up of damp and mould and prevents heat loss through the reduction of more localised extraction systems that require holes to be made in walls that leak in cold air. It also redistributes temperature variations, so helping to heat the home in winter and cool it in the summer. A series of pipes are required to intake and extract air around the home, via the heat recovery unit, which has to be located close to a source of fresh air such as the attic.

WIND TURBINES

Wind turbines use a system of propellers to convert energy from the wind into electricity. These can be either positioned on a tall mast away from any buildings or mounted on a roof. In general, they are mounted on a tower above building height in order to catch the faster moving streams of wind. The wind turbine must be free from obstructions, such as buildings or trees, and ideally located in an area that has a good consistent average wind speed. Before you invest in one, it is worth measuring the average wind speed of your area with an anemometer (wind speed gauge) for as long as possible – preferably over one year – as the more wind that can be harvested, the more electricity will be produced. Alternatively, meteorological offices will hold information on local wind speeds. An average wind speed of at least 6 metres per second is needed to make a wind turbine viable;

Power output does vary depending upon the size of the turbine, however a typical domestic model will create between 1 and 6 kilowatts. As with photovoltaic panels, turbines can also be connected to the National Grid, which means that you can actually sell any excess energy back to the electricity companies via a special inverter and meter system.

Although the presence of a wind turbine is a pleasure for some, others are quite set against

them and any noise that they may produce, hence you may need planning permission from your local authority in order to install one.

BIOMASS HEATERS

Biomass boilers draw energy from natural materials; using either wood in the form of chippings and pre-made wood pellets of fast growing trees like willow, or animal waste and high-energy crops such as sugar cane or maize. The former is more commonly used in domestic situations – I for one would really not want to store a whole load of animal droppings at home.

These natural fuels can be used in a small, stand-alone stove such as a wood burner (some of which can be fitted with a water-heating back boiler) or a more conventional style boiler that has a large storage container (or hopper) to gradually feed in the fuel supply, though these do need to have adequate space planned out.

A biomass heater will supply you with a very low CO_2-producing heating system as you will only be re-emitting the CO_2 already soaked up by the material in its production.

MATERIALS

ECO MATERIALS

TOO MANY PEOPLE HOLD THE FALSE VIEW THAT IMPLEMENTING AN ENVIRONMENTALLY FRIENDLY DESIGN WILL INEVITABLY LEAD TO A COMPROMISE IN STYLE; A LIMITED UNDERSTANDING OF THE AVAILABLE ECO MATERIALS SERVES ONLY TO COMPOUND THIS MISCONCEPTION.

Traditional eco materials such as hemp, lime plaster and sheep's wool are considered by many to be coarse, non-durable and outdated. But beyond the traditional, there is a new generation of advanced materials that not only hold excellent sustainable credentials but also have a wonderful tactile quality and can help our homes to become stylishly eco chic.

Understanding eco materials – what the options are, how they are made, how to use them – is key to creating a home that is at once functional, beautiful and environmentally aware. This chapter opens up the creative possibilities to those who wish to design eco interiors but will not compromise on style.

All too often, when I see eco homes I despair at a heavy-handed reliance on a single material, such as timber, which actually diminishes the design and detracts from the quality of the material; sometimes you metaphorically cannot see the wood for the trees. Using a combination of different materials – and you do not need that many – can help to separate or 'zone' particular spaces as well as providing an opportunity to create focus or drama.

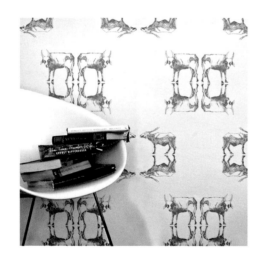

ABOVE Using an eco wallpaper can help you to reduce your home's toxin levels by cutting out petrochemical-laden paints and inks.

As a basic overview, there is a common aspect to each category of eco materials, from the factory-made and technologically advanced, through the natural and sustainable, to the vintage and recycled. By understanding the nature of each category, you can appreciate the way an urban eco chic interior can be brought together – layering surface finishes to create a complete look without an over-reliance on any single material.

An interior that relies solely on technological materials can lack character; furnished only with sleek surfaces, a space can be devoid of real focus. Just think back to those gleaming white kitchens of science fiction films to be reminded of how soulless an interior can be. However, technologically advanced materials can provide a backdrop for natural and recycled materials to come to the fore and be truly appreciated; they can act as the canvas on which the artwork is grounded.

Likewise, if an interior employs too much of one specific natural material – for example, timber – it can be equally overwhelming. This may be fine in a log cabin, but for a more acutely stylish interior, the ideal is a contrast of textures, with technological and vintage materials highlighting the warmth and irregular qualities that a natural product such as wood has to offer.

When an interior is filled with vintage materials and recycled pieces, it is often full of quirky character, but it may languish in nostalgia. A heavy reliance on vintage can point to a lack of ambition to create a truly contemporary space. The layers of age and the piecemeal quality of recycled materials can feel tired and stuffy – as if a fear of the here and now has taken hold.

Balance underpins urban eco chic, combining technology to create clean, efficient spaces; nature to give a grounding warmth and texture; and vintage elements to impart identity and soul. In this way, you can create liveable interiors that are as functional as they are good looking, as healthy as they are environmentally conscious. Now that is what I call urban eco chic.

The following sections within this chapter present a choice of the most stylish eco materials currently available. Alongside each description, I have stated which category of the urban eco chic principle the material sits within – indicating the stylistic effect it will have. This will help you to achieve the desired balance between technology, nature and vintage.

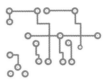

MATERIAL **PARTS**

IN ACCORDANCE WITH THE URBAN ECO CHIC TRIUMVIRATE, ECO MATERIALS FIT BROADLY INTO THE TECHNOLOGY, NATURE OR VINTAGE CATEGORIES. EACH HAS ITS OWN UNIQUE CHARACTERISTICS, WHICH ARE DESCRIBED HERE, AND CAN BE USED IN VARYING RATIOS, DEPENDING ON THE ROOM BEING DECORATED, TO CREATE THE PERFECT ECO CHIC INTERIOR.

TECHNOLOGICALLY ADVANCED ECO MATERIALS

Such materials are often factory made, with a high quality of finish, offering a clean, crisp and contemporary style. They may well look like many other conventional products, but these eco materials will have been made using low-energy techniques or technologically advanced methods that use natural or recycled materials in their content.

Technologically developed materials add a level of precision to your home, which can create a perfect backdrop and textural contrast to natural and vintage materials and objects. In many cases they can also help to reduce your energy or resource usage during their lifespan. This can counteract the relatively high level of embodied energy (see page 51) created in their manufacture, transportation and fitting.

Materials such as linoleum, bio-polymer resins and layered insulating sheet are all examples of technologically advanced materials. You can specify any of these products confident that its performance, reliability and environmental footprint have been carefully considered.

NATURAL OR SUSTAINABLE ECO MATERIALS

When well managed, naturally occurring eco materials are easily replenished, thereby minimising their environmental impact. Materials such as wood, wool, cork and bamboo are excellent examples of natural materials that can be produced in a sustainable manner and benefit the home.

Prone to surface variations in both colour and texture, natural materials have a unique or bespoke quality, adding a material richness to an interior. Generally they have a grain or fibre, which is an inherent part of their character. From a design perspective, natural materials lend a grounding quality to a space, offering a relaxing warmth, which helps us to reconnect with ourselves and nature as a whole. Unlike many artificial products, natural materials such as wood and leather age well, gaining character with use.

When left untreated by chemical finishes, natural materials are free from toxins that can off-gas. Some may even have natural anti-bacterial qualities. As a further benefit, they will be breathable, allowing moisture to pass through, and so help to manage condensation and the prevention of damp within the home.

VINTAGE AND RECYCLED ECO MATERIALS

Using vintage items within an interior scheme is, in my opinion, a valid form of recycling for you are saving perfectly serviceable materials or furniture from entering landfill. But there are, of course, more conventional recycled materials that are created anew from discarded items.

Recycled materials frequently wear their eco credentials on their sleeves, so can be easily identified. Made from reprocessed products, they often take on a mottled appearance. As recycling processes improve, the quality and design of such materials are becoming more refined. Instead of being made up of a dozen or more contrasting coloured parts, they can consist of fewer tonal shades, offering a different and, for some, more visually pleasing look.

Products labelled as recycled may be made up of a relatively low percentage of reprocessed materials. Manufacturers may apply the term when a product has a recycled content of 40% or more, with up to 60% being made up of new materials. For me, this figure is too low.

Materials that are easily recyclable, such as polypropylene, also fall within this category. Ease of recyclability may indicate a high recycled content, but not always. Materials with a high recycled content and easy recyclability include glass stone, stainless steel and some plastics.

ABOVE When I came to decorate my own living room, the eco-credentials of each material were foremost in my mind – from the eco-friendly paints applied to the walls to the recycled glass stone used to create the kitchen surfaces and the round tabletop.

ECO CRITERIA

No matter which category – technology, nature or vintage – an eco material falls into, when discussing it, there are key terms to be aware of:

EMBODIED ENERGY is the energy taken to extract, produce, transport and fit a material to the point of its intended use. Measured in kilowatt hours per metre cubed (kWh/m^3), these calculations enable us to compare the relative environmental merits of materials and products. If steel is shipped a vast distance from its place of manufacture, it will have a high embodied energy compared with locally sourced timber, which will have a low embodied energy. Although difficult to calculate accurately, it is necessary to have a comparative index of the environmental impact of materials.

LIFE CYCLE ANALYSIS takes into account not only the embodied energy of a material but its whole life cost, from production, through usage and, finally, disposal. This analysis helps us understand how great an impact each material has on the environment, taking into account its durability and recyclability.

CRADLE-TO-CRADLE materials are those considered from an environmental perspective throughout their life cycle – in other words, a material that is produced in a well-managed, sustainable manner from a renewable source, used efficiently and then recycled easily at the end of its useful life, ready to become a raw material for another use. By contrast, if the life cycle of a material is not considered, it will finally – and wastefully – be put into landfill; so this is known as a cradle-to-grave material.

ECO FLOORS

WHEN CHOOSING YOUR IDEAL
FLOORING, YOU WILL BE
BALANCING FUNCTION AND
STYLE WITH COST, AS FLOOR
AREAS MAKE A SUBSTANTIAL
IMPACT ON ANY BUDGET.
ALSO, IT WILL NOT SURPRISE
YOU TO LEARN THAT FLOORS
AFFECT THE ENVIRONMENTAL
IMPACT OF YOUR HOME –
BOTH INSIDE AND OUT.

Within the home, flooring surfaces can absorb warmth from the sun – good in winter bad in summer – or insulate against heat loss. Their colour and surface texture can bounce light around a space, cutting back on the need for artificial light. The correct flooring materials may also improve air quality, enhancing a 'healthy' home whereas the wrong surfaces may trap dust, aggrevate allergies and release toxins over time.

Similarly, your choice of floor materials affects the environment outside your home. For instance, choosing a hardwood floor may contribute to the destruction of delicate ecosystems or fund illegal logging practices. The production of plastics may create unnecessary levels of pollution, whilst their transportation from far-flung locations contributes to a higher carbon footprint.

Lastly, their disposal (and cheaper flooring may not last as long) may release trapped toxins into the environment during the degrading process at landfill. Encouragingly, there are a surprising number of beautiful environmentally conscious flooring options for every style, budget and spatial concept – so you need not feel limited.

OPPOSITE A selection of eco flooring solutions (clockwise from top left) natural pebble tiles, bamboo, FSC-certified timber, cork tiles, sisal and recycled rubber.

LINOLEUM

Linoleum – or lino – is made from natural, renewable materials including linseed oil, wood or cork flour and flax, laid onto a natural fibre backing such as canvas or hessian.

It has no artificial chemicals, so is good for keeping toxin levels low. Being a hardwearing smooth surface, it is easy to clean without trapping dust. It also has a natural anti-bacterial agent: it off-gases linseed oil, which exterminates germs but is non-toxic to humans.

Linoleum is available in a range of colours in both a continuous roll, to create seamless surfaces, and as individual tiles, which can be laid in a variety of patterns. It is an ideal material for kitchens, bathrooms, hallways and any other spaces that come into regular contact with water.

NATURAL RUBBER

Natural rubber flooring is made from the latex sap of rubber trees, which is extracted by scoring the bark and allowing the sap to seep out. Once collected, the yellow latex is mixed with other natural materials and pigments before being heated, pressure treated and finally cut into tiles. Offcuts from factories are conveniently recycled: they are shredded and mixed to create flooring for sports facilities and also acoustic and thermal insulation.

Only 10% of rubber flooring on the market is natural. Manufacturers claim it is a carbon-positive material because rubber trees take so much carbon from the atmosphere as they grow that this outweighs any put back through its manufacture and transportation. Natural rubber gives off no toxic fumes.

Available in a wide variety of colours and surface textures, natural rubber flooring has great design potential. It is often used in primary colours and so can feel hi-tech or even playful and naïve. But if specified with a smooth surface and in a natural, muted shade, it can feel more sophisticated, which makes it perfect for urban kitchens and bathrooms.

Being highly durable, waterproof and easy to clean, natural rubber, like lino, can be used in wet spaces and areas of high traffic, such as hallways.

A textured surface makes natural rubber non-slip, and also absorbs impact and noise. However, it can sustain dents if furniture is placed directly on top of it and scuffs can show up on the smoother types.

RECYCLED RUBBER

Recycled rubber floors are made of both post-industrial and virgin rubber chips.

Like the other rubber products, it is available as tiles or in rolls and must be laid directly onto a smooth floor surface, using adhesive.

Available in a limited range of neutral colours, recycled rubber flooring has (as with many recycled materials) a mottled quality when seen in close proximity. Due to its mixed contents, variations in colour do occur, but since the surface is formed of different coloured chips, this is barely noticeable.

Tough, durable and with good non-slip qualities, recycled rubber flooring is ideal for areas of high traffic. However, this material does yellow when exposed to direct sunlight.

RECYCLED RUBBER MATTING

Worn bus tyres are difficult to dispose of in an environmentally friendly manner. However, a manufacturer in the United States has developed a process whereby these tyres are chopped up and wire-brushed down to expose the nylon fibres they contain (in Europe, steel wire reinforcements are used). The resulting material is then bonded together (although, sadly, with a polyurethane glue) to create a chenille-like mosaic of recycled rubber matting.

Its extended life makes it a good environmental choice and an alternative to the conventional polypropylene, but it does have a high embodied energy within its production. For customers outside the United States, its carbon footprint is increased because of the transportation involved.

Available as carpet tile squares or in rolls, the matting comes in a variety of colours, all with a black rubber background. This flooring is incredibly durable and surprisingly soft, which makes it useful in high traffic areas. Being made of rubber, it can be used both inside and out.

CARPET TILES

Various methods are used to produce carpet tiles, but typically fibres are tufted onto a natural fibre backing material, such as hemp, cotton or linen, which is then coated with latex to hold the fibres in place. Lastly, a bitumen backing is applied to give the tile strength and rigidity.

Although they have a relatively high embodied energy due to their production, carpet tiles are long lasting and can be reconditioned and reused. If discarded, they can be burnt to produce energy.

Carpet tiles are extremely hardwearing and can simply be replaced when worn or damaged. They are easy to install and can be laid straight onto a floor using double-sided tape or a special adhesive, cutting the expense of fitting. Since they can be laid individually, carpet tiles are a flexible option in difficult-to-access areas. A familiar sight in offices, their ever more sophisticated range of colours and styles makes them a real option for the home.

PAPER RUGS

Paper rugs are stronger and more hardwearing than you might imagine. Fabricated solely from sustainable materials, they are made from the soft wood pulp of coniferous trees. The paper is mixed with a resin and then made into a yarn, which is woven onto a natural jute or latex backing.

They are available in a selection of natural soft browns to greys with a greater variety of broader trim colours. Despite being flexible and durable they are best used in areas of light to medium footfall, but not on stairways or under furniture on castors.

ABOVE These simple wooden floorboards add rustic character to this bedroom, providing a textural backdrop for the clean lines of the bed and other furniture.

CORK

Cut by hand from the bark of the cork oak tree, cork actually grows back over 8–10 years when it is ready for further harvesting. It truly is a sensational sustainable material, and a firm favourite of designers from the early modernists of the 1920s to the present day.

Cork has a closed-cell honeycomb-like structure, which makes it warm to the touch, water resistant and a good thermal insulator and gives it natural bounce. Beside being easy to clean, cork is durable, with a natural insect resistance called suberin and an anti-allergenic quality. All these properties make it a great choice for domestic flooring.

Cork flooring is available as square tiles and also laminated to a timber sub base to create click-together planks. Dyed either dark or lighter natural shades, cork can create a luxurious effect with the added benefit that the paler shades help to reflect light back into a space.

Conventionally used in bathrooms and kitchens, cork is now chic enough to be used in bedrooms and living rooms as well.

BAMBOO

Bamboo is a grass; so when it is harvested, its roots simply re-grow another shoot, dispensing with the need to replant seeds and preventing soil erosion. It grows at exceptional speed – as opposed to 15–25 years for timber, bamboo is ready to cut in 3–5 years – without the need for pesticides.

Planks are made from the solid outer edges of the bamboo stalk, which is cut into very precise thin strips and laminated together to form solid boards. The tight grain structure creates a tough surface, and the laminated strips can lie horizontally or vertically. When they are laid horizontally, the regular rhythm of the bamboo knots is shown, whereas laid vertically they produce a smooth knot-free floor. For higher traffic areas, bamboo can be turned into a thin thread, which is bonded together with a resin to create a floor that is twice as tough and resistant to the impact of even stiletto heels.

Bamboo is available only in a limited colour range and generally comes with a pre-finished lacquer, so you cannot stain it yourself. Due to its speed of growth and availability, bamboo is more affordable than hardwood, which makes it one of the cheapest natural floorings available. The only drawback is that production is largely in the Far East, so it has a higher embodied energy through transporation than a locally sourced timber floor.

TIMBER

All timber products should be sourced from a sustainable, well-managed supply. One of the most widely recognised groups that certify sustainable management is the Forest Stewardship Council (FSC). Buying FSC-certified timber and products supports the environmentally responsible, socially beneficial and economically viable management of the world's forests. It ensures the protection not only of the forest itself but also of the huge biodiversity affected by logging. If not carefully managed, logging can have a disastrous effect on a forest and, on a greater scale, global climate change. This book is printed on paper from FSC-certified timber, so see page 4 for the FSC logo.

By replacing high-embodied-energy materials such as steel, the use of wood can reduce the carbon footprint of homes and the number of toxins present within them. Moreover, wood is a biodegradable material that, when used thoughtfully, can be recycled or will decompose naturally.

SOLID TIMBER

A familiar material to us all, solid timber flooring brings a natural warmth to any home. Its textural quality is grounding and calming. To reduce the carbon footprint of the timber, it should ideally be from as local a source as possible and not the other side of the globe.

Timber floors are available as soft- or hardwood planks, tongue-and-groove boards and parquet tiles. Many beautiful timber floors are supplied pre-finished with a lacquer or polyurethane coating, which can contain off-gassing VOCs, so check before you buy. The natural beauty of timber is best brought out through the use of natural waxes and oils, such as Danish oil, which give it a soft lustre with no off-gassing toxins. Buy the flooring unfinished and treat it yourself. Although it is very hardwearing, solid timber is prone to scratches and dents; but as with any solid material, the marks can be sanded out.

Finally, as a natural material, timber is prone to expansion and shrinkage, depending on moisture conditions. Leave timber in your home for up to two weeks prior to fitting to ensure it is acclimatised.

ENGINEERED TIMBER

Made from layers of a combination of soft- and hardwoods, engineered timber floors have advantages and disadvantages over those made from solid timber. On the plus side, they can be made up of entirely FSC-certified wood using only a small quantity of slower-growing hardwood and a base layer of less expensive softwood, taken from faster-growing forests. Also, the base layer can be made from smaller pieces than the surface layer, so it is a more efficient use of the wood and reduces waste.

As a composite, engineered timber has flexibility in terms of available sizes and is less prone to the effects of humidity and warping than solid timber. If dented, engineered timber can be sanded down and refinished, though the result depends on the depth of the dent and that of the top hardwood layer.

On the downside, engineered timber does not have as long a lifespan as solid wood. Also it has a higher embodied energy due to the manufacturing process. Because of its greater number of component parts, it is also harder to recycle and cannot be reused so readily. Lastly, the bonding agent is likely to be a formaldehyde resin glue, which will, over time, off-gas toxins into your home. So if it were my home, I would opt for the solid timber flooring and swallow the extra cost.

STONE TILES

Provided they are cut from a local source, stone tiles are a viable environmental material. As a naturally occurring substance, stone is mined from the earth, cut and then polished; no carbon-heavy firing process is necessary, as it is with ceramic tiles. Stone can be recycled at the end of its useful life; crushed into smaller pieces, it can be reused within the building industry. Even when deposited in landfill, stone remains inert – it does not produce toxins or release methane. Shipping stone tiles vast distances massively increases its embodied energy, so look online to see what types of stone are mined locally to you and work this into your interior scheme.

Stone tiles have a natural, variegated colour and surface texture; the material's strength gives durability and longevity wherever it is used. If you have only a small floor area to tile, search reclamation yards and salvage sites for materials that may be left over from other building projects that you can buy cheaply.

With stone it is best to specify a honed finish, which gives it a softer, matt look, to bring out the natural quality of the surface. A highly polished gloss finish can make stone look as though it has been coated with a shiny polyurethane layer.

PEBBLE TILES

Simple, soft rounded pebbles are collected by hand from beaches in India and Indonesia, their bases ground flat and fixed with adhesive to a backing sheet to form tiles. Once laid and grouted, the tiles' smooth surface and natural colour variations work to create a calm feel within a space.

Although these pebble tiles have a low-level manufacturing energy attached to them, they are transported vast distances from their point of manufacture, which increases their embodied energy. Furthermore, picking pebbles from beaches is not encouraged in many regions, as it can in effect cause coastal erosion.

Once laid with a grout, these tiles cannot be taken up and reused. However, as a natural material that requires no surface finish or colouration, if put in landfill they are relatively inert and so will not break down to create any polluting toxins.

Being textural yet so hardwearing, these natural pebble tiles work brilliantly in areas of high traffic, such as hallways. But they are also a good choice where a bit of sensory impact is desirable – for example, in a bathroom.

RIGHT This vintage rug ties in with the well-travelled suitcases and wool throws, plus it provides a warm surface to step onto when getting in and out of bed. Due to its age, it is unlikely to have been treated with the cocktail of toxins that modern rugs often contain.

RUGS

In order to reduce the effects of dust and mites, combine hard flooring with a softer surface, such as a natural or vintage rug, which can be used to zone an area within a room. Most of the natural floorcoverings mentioned in this section, such as sisal and coir, can be made into an edged rug. Rather than pay over the odds for a custom-made rug, buy a piece of natural flooring to fit the dimensions of your space and have it finished with a fabric or leather trim.

Another option is ethnic rugs. If you are happy to live with their colourful style, it is worth remembering that hand-made ethnic rugs crafted in remote areas may well not have been treated with the normal cocktail of commercial fire retardants and chemicals. An alternative is to buy vintage or antique rugs from markets or antique shops, which may well have been made before the introduction of fire retardants. Their age and wear add character to your home and a sense of luxury or nostalgia.

NATURAL WOOL CARPET

Pure wool fibres – the history of which should be checked for any possible chemical contamination – are woven onto a natural fibre backing, such as linen or cotton, which in turn is backed with a natural latex rubber. But be sure to specify 100% *natural* wool carpet and not simply 100% wool carpet as the latter may contain toxins in its artificial latex backing.

Unlike artificial fibres, sheep's wool fleece contains lanolin, which acts as a natural stain inhibitor; due its ability to absorb moisture, the

LEFT Parquet flooring creates a hardwearing yet warm reception floor. The wood can easily be reused, extending its useful life.

BELOW Coir natural flooring is a sophisticated choice of covering. Whilst coir is not as soft underfoot as wool, it is warmer to the touch than a solid wood or stone floor surface and helps to reduce any noise transmission to the space below.

fleece is also naturally anti-static. At the end of its useful life, pure wool carpet will biodegrade without harm to the environment.

Pure natural wool carpet is perhaps the most hardwearing and easy to maintain of all the natural soft flooring materials. On the whole, pure natural wool carpets are available in either chunky or fine pile (for a more contemporary feel) and in a selection of natural shades. Soft and warm underfoot, it is perfect for hallways, bedrooms and living rooms. As an alternative, pure wool can be blended with flax or sisal to create floor coverings with a fine weave, texture and strength. A wool-flax blend is softer underfoot whilst a wool-sisal blend creates a tweed effect.

With all natural floorcoverings, manufacturers recommend using a stain-protection solution at the point of fitting. Natural materials do not react well to water and can mark, so it is important to be aware of the cleaning instructions the moment the flooring is fitted – do not wait for a spillage! Most manufacturers will sell you a care kit, which may prove to be good value; it will certainly be cheaper than replacing a marked carpet.

SISAL

Grown in Africa and South America, sisal is extracted from the agave cactus plant and has traditionally been used in rope making. Sisal is likely to be toxin free and it uses no artificial backing materials, which may contaminate it. Similar to wool, it is anti-static and will bio-degrade at the end of its life.

It is hardwearing, but coarser to the touch than wool, which makes it a good choice for hallways and stairs. It is available in a wide range of weaves – from herringbone to bouclé – and in natural colours.

COIR

Coir is made in India from the fibres of coconut husks. These are removed by hand, washed and softened before being woven into a flooring material, after which a latex backing is applied.

Coir is coarse in texture and rough to the touch but it is hardwearing and appropriate for use in living rooms and hallways. The threads are chunky and can appear hairy, so it is not a clean contemporary look. It is available in just a small range of colours and weaves, but it is considered to be good value.

JUTE

The stalk of the corchorus plant, in southern India, provides the basis of jute. It has a fine woven texture with a soft sheen. As the least hardwearing of the natural fibre floorcoverings, it is better suited to low traffic areas such as living rooms and bedrooms. It is available in just a small selection of shades and weaves.

SEAGRASS AND MOUNTAIN GRASS

Both seagrass and mountain grass are available as natural fibre floorings. Although they are affordable, they are not widely used. Often they have wide weaves with a shiny surface texture, which makes them slippery and thus inappropriate for use in areas such as stairways, but usable in living rooms, dining rooms and bedrooms. They are available in a narrow selection of weaves and natural colours, in shades of light brown.

RECLAIMED TIMBER PLANKS AND PARQUET

A vast amount of the timber we consume each year heads straight to landfill, where it produces methane – a gas three times more harmful to the environment than CO_2. So finding alternative uses for wood salvaged from old buildings and the construction industry makes far more sense, especially when it is so highly reusable. Diverting timber from landfill reduces the need for new wood to be felled and transported, and with it unnecessary carbon emissions.

Because timber ages well, you are buying a material with an identity that adds depth to interior spaces. Use it on floors, walls, worksurfaces, in fact anywhere you might use conventional timber. You have the option of using it either in its original state with an aged surface finish – knocks, dents and all – or sanding it back to reveal a fresh surface finish.

Unless you have a guaranteed supply from an old building under demolition, using reclaimed timber flooring is something of a lottery: it is a question of what is available at the time you need it. Due to its age and reuse, there is a possibility of woodworm and other damage, so inspect it carefully and treat as appropriate. Search for reclaimed timber and parquet blocks online or, even better, at a local wood recycling centre.

ECO WALLS

TREATING YOUR WALLS IS THE EASIEST AND MOST COST-EFFECTIVE WAY TO IMPACT ON THE LOOK AND FEEL OF A SPACE. BUT EVEN A SEEMINGLY SIMPLE PAINT JOB HAS ENVIRONMENTAL CONSEQUENCES BOTH WITHIN YOUR HOME AND ON THE WIDER WORLD OUTSIDE IT.

Using environmentally friendly wall finishes need not limit what you can do within an interior space, for there is now an excellent variety of eco materials to work with. Even better, non-toxic and sustainable products bring a number of positive benefits that will enhance your home's urban eco chic feel.

Light-reflective surfaces, such as some recycled plastics, and translucent materials, like glass, can bounce natural light around your home and so reduce the need for additional artificial lighting. Eco wall coverings, including timber and natural-fibre wallpapers, add impact, character and texture, whilst using eco paints keeps your home smelling sweet and toxin free to create a healthier living space.

Ensuring that the materials you use come from a truly sustainable source will mean that when you have finished with them they can either be recycled or will easily biodegrade. By choosing eco wall treatments you are making an enhancement to your home, without sacrificing your personal style, and at the same time showing your commitment to caring for the environment.

OPPOSITE There are a number of exciting environmentally conscious wall treatments to choose from (clockwise from top left) an ingenious internal wall made from recycled glass bottles, recycled plastic panels, eco wallpaper printed with non-toxic inks, oiled timber boards, recycled glass tiles and ecoresin sheets – this one encases natural reeds.

ABOVE Contemporary design does not need to be all sharp edges and hard geometry; the uneven wall surface in this living room adds a softness that mimics that of the unstructured sofa.

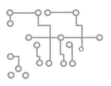

⊙ ECO OR NATURAL PAINT

Made from a variety of materials, including water, chalk, limestone, natural oils and clays, natural paints coat walls in breathable, non-toxic colour.

Conventional paints use petrochemical products, so not only are they pollution heavy, toxins are also generated during their manufacture. Toxic solvents used in conventional paints to improve paint flow are known collectively as Volatile Organic Compounds (VOCs). These solvents evaporate off as paint dries and for some time after. Where conventional paints are used and there is insufficient ventilation, VOCs can cause headaches, dizziness and nausea, breathing difficulties and allergic reactions. All paint tins must now display their VOC content.

Toxin- and VOC-free paints are available in a wide range of colours. They are durable, low odour and contain zero toxins, which means freshly decorated rooms may be immediately inhabited. Used in identical ways to conventional paints, applied with a brush or roller, they require the same preparation.

Technically advanced clay paints are an alternative to water-based emulsions. Their high clay content means the paint is thick enough to be applied in one coat, covers small cracks, does not splatter and gives a smooth, matt finish. VOC-free clay paints are breathable, allowing moisture to move through walls, preventing damp and saving paint surfaces from cracking. Trapped moisture within walls can lead to a damaging build-up of damp, which in turn can promote fungal growths such as mildew. So breathable clay paints are better for your home – particularly timber-framed structures – and health.

Likewise, lime wash is a breathable wall coating. An old-fashioned paint with a chalky finish, lime wash is made from crushed limestone and water mixed with pigments to create soft, pastel shades. The lime is naturally anti-bacterial and insecticidal so is a good repellent for bugs and woodworm.

As well as clay paint, natural coatings are available as emulsion, eggshell, lime wash and a range of varnishes, lacquers and oils. With their quality now comparable to conventional paints there seems little reason – apart from their slightly higher financial cost – not to use eco or natural paints. But what price do you put on the health of your family and the people around you?

LIME PLASTER

After a lull in popularity, lime plaster has returned to the fore as a building material because it is porous, allowing moisture to seep in and evaporate out.

Lime plaster can be used on interior walls in conjunction with breathable finishes such as clay paints. Use lime plaster when re-pointing brickwork to prevent the bricks from retaining moisture and losing their protective face. Lime plaster and mortars are soft and allow for movement, self-heal any small cracks and ultimately can be removed so the bricks may then be reused.

GLASS

Although glass has a high embodied energy due to the carbon-heavy manufacturing processes and its weight, glass panels allow natural light to filter through and so reduce the need for artificial lighting. Using glass to create internal partitions within spaces that do not require good acoustic privacy – kitchens, dining rooms, living rooms – makes sense, allowing light to be drawn through the house.

As the angle of the sun's light changes, glass allows you to create dynamic lighting effects. Use glass screens, blocks or partitions anywhere light falls onto walls or the floor.

RECYCLED GLASS TILES

During manufacture, recycled glass is cleaned, crushed and heated until it reaches crystallisation point. At this stage the glass fuses before being left to cool; this adds strength to the outer surface of the tile. Tiles made from coloured glass can retain the original colour – for example, green wine bottles produce green tiles. Tiles made from uncoloured glass are often back-painted in a range of colours.

Whilst they reuse glass that would otherwise go to landfill, these tiles have a high embodied energy due to the recycling process, but arguably less than conventional ceramic tiles. Currently, glass tiles are not widely available. Due to the relatively small scale of production, combined with high labour and manufacturing costs, these tiles can be expensive.

Recycled glass tiles add a contemporary sparkle and translucent quality to kitchens and bathrooms. Although best used on wall surfaces, they can be used on horizontal worksurfaces, but not floors.

RECYCLED PLASTIC

Recycling plastics prevents an incredible array of discarded products from going to landfill. The plastics are sorted, cleaned and chipped into flakes; then, through a combination of heat and pressure, reformed into solid plastic sheets. These sheets have a mottled quality, as the colouration from the recycled materials does not mix. Whilst some sheets are colourful, the mixes can be made subtler.

Each type of recycled plastic has different properties. For example, recycled yoghurt pots produce a hard but smooth plastic with a mottled surface colour, with just the odd fleck of authentic silver foil. It is also good to know that each variety of plastic is again recyclable at the end of its life, which makes it a cradle-to-cradle material.

Decorative recycled plastics work well as splashbacks, cupboard doors, bathroom surfaces and tabletops, but they are not heat resistant and so are inappropriate for kitchen worksurfaces.

ECORESIN™ PANELS

Made from clear plastics – 40% of which are recycled – Varia™ ecoresin™ panels provide a stunning range of wallcoverings. The panels are made up in layers, allowing other materials, such as grasses or flowers, to be incorporated.

Ecoresin™ works wonderfully as backlit panels, tabletops, splashbacks and even partition screens. The textural natural materials added to the resin provide warmth, yet it has almost 40 times the impact resistance of glass. It is also fully recyclable at the end of its life. Currently manufactured only in the United States, transporting these ecoresin™ panels outside that country increases their embodied energy and carbon footprint.

OPPOSITE A home office space that uses predominately natural materials. Such materials could overpower a smaller, more enclosed room; but because this study corner is cleverly positioned in an open-plan, flexible space, the wood cladding simply emphasises the feature wall, while the display shelving adds visual interest.

ABOVE A stylised floral motif wallpaper takes centre stage in this homely and highly personal bedroom. A conventional headboard has been dispensed with, leaving just the simple bed, plainly clothed in a patchwork cover of soft, natural shades.

● RECYCLED COMPOSITES

There are a number of crushed or recycled material composites that can be used as kitchen or bathroom surfaces. These composites use small segments of otherwise unusable materials, including stone, glass and plastics, that are crushed into tiny pieces before being bonded together in a resin (ideally solvent free) to create solid, zero-maintenance surfaces. Not only can these composites be moulded to a specific size but additional pieces can be seamlessly joined on during the manufacturing process, allowing chic-looking integral sinks to be added.

Being recycled these composites have a mottled surface, but are generally available in a variety of colours. This material has a fresh sparkle to it as the light catches the particles close to the surface, which contrasts wonderfully with natural materials, such as wood.

TIMBER CLADDING

Also known as tongue-and-groove boarding, timber cladding is similar to solid wood flooring except, as it does not bear any weight, it is thinner – generally ranging between 7.5–9mm thick. Timber wall cladding is available in several different profiles, from a plain style to more decorative designs. The v-shaped grooves of the cladding add rhythm to a space, the nature of the timber absorbing any acoustic noise. It is likely to be made from a soft wood, so ensure whatever you select comes from a FSC-certified source.

When fitting timber wall cladding, it is best to leave it in the space to acclimatise and shrink for two weeks prior to fixing in order to prevent gaps from forming. Fit the panelling to a series of battens screwed to the wall at spaces of 40cm, and detail the cladding carefully around any electrical and plumbing fittings.

When applied to walls, timber cladding can either be painted or left its natural colour. Unadorned the wood surface lends a soft, rustic effect to a room, akin to a log cabin. The wood should be oiled for protection whilst allowing the timber to breathe. Alternatively, painting the cladding prevents it from visibly aging and warming in colour. Depending on your chosen shade and finish, a variety of effects from a gentle Scandinavian style through to a seaside beach hut feel can be created – just be sure to use a breathable, VOC-free paint.

RECLAIMED TIMBER CLADDING

Over the last couple of years I have experimented with cladding walls with reclaimed floorboards. Handled carefully, this treatment can combine a natural material with a contemporary finish. The age and warmth of textured timber imbues any room with atmosphere and acts as a focal point within the space. If you can find aged fencing panels (that have not had bitumen or creosote applied to them) their silvered finish will look wonderful.

Source timber floorboards from reclamation yards and clean them very gently with a wire brush or mild soap and water to retain their character. Timber expands and shrinks, so it is best to let the boards acclimatise to your home for a few days before fitting them onto the walls, using screws and battens. They can then be left natural, oiled or even dragged with natural paint to give them a gentle, aged feel.

ECO WALLPAPER

Environmentally friendly wallpapers are now easy to source in a wide range of decorative designs. Made from 100% FSC-certified timber or with a high percentage of recycled paper fibres, the paper pulp is made with long fibres so that it withstands wet adhesive and stays strong. The paper is printed with vegetable inks, left to dry and then packaged in biodegradable materials.

Eco wallpapers harbour no embedded toxins, so it is a healthy product to use in your home. It can be hung using natural starch adhesives and will neither fade nor discolour; the average lifespan of an eco wallpaper is between five and six years (the time period after which you might wish to redecorate anyway). At the end of its usable life, eco wallpaper degrades completely, without polluting the environment.

As these papers have no surface coating, they may not be used in wet areas such as bathrooms or kitchens; however, they are great for use elsewhere. They make good feature walls and work well when accompanied by a paint scheme that matches the background colour of the paper, allowing the pattern to stand out and paper to blend in.

An alternative is natural wallpapers, which are available in a variety of surface finishes, from sisal to sea grass, bamboo to arrowroot. These papers may well have ingredients that have travelled long distances, but they will bring sophistication, natural warmth and texture to your walls. However, they can be fragile, so are perhaps best kept for areas of low traffic to minimise wear and tear.

ECO SURFACES

OF ALL THE SURFACES IN THE HOME, DOUBTLESS THE KITCHEN AND BATHROOM SURFACES HAVE THE TOUGHEST ROLES TO PLAY. THEY HAVE TO COPE WITH EXTREMES OF TEMPERATURE AS WELL AS SPILLAGES OF LIQUID, DETERGENTS AND FOOD, YET REMAIN CLEAN AND HYGIENIC.

In addition, surfaces constitute a high percentage cost of any kitchen or bathroom. And, being so visible, they form a key part of the look of the space. So when making your choice of material, which has to fulfil so many critical functions, what comes first? Practicality, cost, or style? If choosing the right surface were not hard enough, I am also asking you to think about the environment when making that decision. As more people reject processed foods in favour of purer produce for health and environmental reasons, it only seems right that the surfaces on which we prepare food reflect this move towards the organic and sustainable. If you are choosing to eat organic and fairtrade, the likelihood is that you are already thinking about eco issues in the kitchen, so why not also in your design choices?

Alongside looks, durability and ease of maintenance, place of origin and toxic content (as a constituent part of the material or applied to the material's surface in the form of a finish) must be considered when choosing the perfect surface. Do also bear in mind that if you decide to refit your kitchen or bathroom and no longer have a use for the surface, that material must go somewhere. Consider all these issues now.

OPPOSITE Eco surfaces range from (clockwise from top left) recycled glass, hand-made mosaics, natural slate, crushed and recycled glass stone, bamboo and recycled plastics.

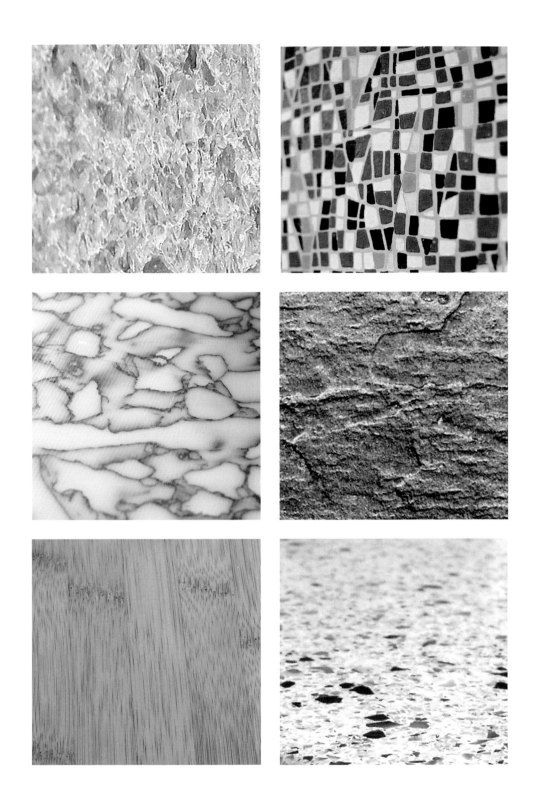

GLASS STONE

Glass stone – also known as Resilica™ – is a composite made up of 85% crushed recycled glass set into solvent-free resin. Made by pouring the glass and resin mixture into a mould, the resulting glass stone is left to set (or cure) for three days after which time it is ground down to thickness and diamond polished to reveal the surface layer glass fragments – a process that can take up to five hours per square metre. The result is a silky smooth terrazzo-like worksurface with fragments of glass that reflect the light but is tough, durable and ideal for kitchens, bathrooms and tabletops.

On the plus side, glass stone is versatile, diverts glass away from landfill, has a high resistance to heat, stains and scratches and is low maintenance. On the negative side, all the hard work and time in producing glass stone is reflected in its high cost, similar to that of a natural stone.

Glass stone is an exciting alternative to solid stone or plastic and is available in a dazzling choice of colours. It can either be coordinated with the rest of the kitchen or used to create an impact with intense colour. But just remember that strong colours are very personal, while lighter surfaces will reflect more light into a space.

DURAT®

Durat® is a man-made material with a high recycled plastics content and is itself 100% recyclable. As it is a solid core material – in other words, it is the same material and colour all the way through – if it does get scratched or marked, it can simply be sanded back, thereby extending its lifespan in areas of high use. Its downside is that, depending on where you live, Durat® may have a high carbon footprint, as the plastics are collected in Scandinavia where it is manufactured.

Durat® has a silky finish with a subtle sparkle to it, and is available in an exciting range of colours. The real bonus with Durat® is that lengths of it can be seamlessly welded together, so that you can create as long a section of it as you like. For a professional finish you can integrate sinks and basins into the work surfaces, welding the material on and hiding any join lines.

STAINLESS STEEL

Whilst it may be too harsh for other areas of the home, stainless steel is perfect for the hardwearing kitchen – it is durable, easy to clean and light reflective. It also lends an air of the 'professional chef' to your kitchen.

Stainless steel can be ordered new and tailored to your space; it needs careful measuring and maybe a template to ensure an exact fit. Its inherent toughness and anti-corrosion surface coating means that stainless steel cannot be cut down on site if it is the wrong size. As a new material, stainless steel contains around 50% recycled material and is itself 100% recyclable, so at the end of its useful life it can be disposed of responsibly.

This high level of durability allows stainless steel freestanding units to be reused again and again: when you move home, it is possible to take these kitchen units with you to the new property. Reclamation yards often have a steady supply of units from professional kitchens ready to be wiped over and reused. Instead of going for the super-sleek (and occasionally characterless) fully fitted kitchen, opt for freestanding cabinets or even a mixture of both to give your kitchen a freer, funky feel. These pieces contrast wonderfully with natural timber or crisply painted surfaces. At the end of their useful life, stainless steel units can be taken back to the yard where they came from or sold on to a dealer as scrap metal.

TIMBER

Locally sourced solid timber is the obvious wholesome choice for an eco kitchen or bathroom. It has a wonderfully warm and tactile surface with a soft directional grain, which makes each piece unique. Timber is hardwearing, durable and in many respects improves with age. What is more, unlike artificial materials where bacteria are free to reproduce, wood contains natural enzymes that fight unwanted bacteria, making it a healthier option for your home.

Because it is not stain resistant, timber needs regular maintenance. Luckily, wood can be sanded back to remove any marks, thereby having a

ABOVE Bathroom surfaces need to be durable, waterproof and easy to clean. The natural pebble floor tiles and geometric unglazed wall tiles are softened by the use of the oiled, sustainble oak basin plinth.

RIGHT This glass stone surface is made up of 85% crushed recycled glass in a solvent-free resin, creating a smooth, sleek surface that really sparkles in the sunlight.

ABOVE Stainless steel can be made with a high content of recycled materials and can itself be recycled. The hard lines of this professional-style kitchen are softened by the vintage chairs and open display shelves.

potentially long lifespan. Ideally wooden surfaces should be oiled or waxed – rather than varnished – once a year to retain their natural feel. Polyurethane varnish simply coats the timber in shiny layers and denies the wood's true quality, and can leak toxins into your home.

If you already have wooden cabinet doors, you should choose a different material for the work surfaces as it can be frustratingly difficult to match the woods precisely, and they will age differently over time. Contrasting materials will break up horizontal and vertical surfaces and set up exciting visual contrasts. Conversely, if you are considering a timber surface, match it with either glass-fronted or spray-painted cabinet doors.

Whichever timber surface you choose, it is critical that you opt for FSC-certified wood. Then at the end of its useful life the timber can be recycled, becoming a cradle-to-cradle material. It can be either sanded and reused or chipped and then left to biodegrade or used to form timber byproducts, such as chipboard.

BAMBOO
An eco alternative to large sections of timber is bamboo (see also page 57). Once cut and harvested, small sections of bamboo are laminated together to create solid worksurface-size boards.

Bamboo has a natural anti-bacterial quality, which is a useful property for a worksurface. It is naturally light brown, but can be stained or simply finished with a Danish oil to protect it from wear and tear while retaining the material's natural texture and warmth. The drawback to this material is that most bamboo is grown in the Far East; so it can have a high embodied energy due to the distance it must be transported.

NATURAL STONE
Again the main eco issue with stone is that it is extremely heavy and often must travel far, thereby massively adding to its carbon footprint (see also page 58). The only true eco option is to avoid stone altogether, unless it is sourced from your own country and, ideally, locally.

Often stone is polished to a sleek, high gloss finish, but I find this can give it a cheap plastic quality, which diminishes the stone's natural texture. Instead opt for a honed (soft sheen) finish, which will keep the stone's wonderful tactile quality. Stone surfaces will need to be sealed before use, so check that the sealant does not contain VOCs or other toxins that can off-gas into your home.

RECYCLED TIMBER
A trip to your local reclamation yard can yield some exciting discoveries. Whilst it relies on chance, if you are persistent, real gems do turn up. Reclaimed oak or teak tabletops and science lab desks from schools and universities can often be sourced, providing tough, durable surfaces with lots of character. They can be sanded down, or cleaned up or in some cases just left as they are – the wear and tear adding character to the final design.

MOSAICS
Making use of small or chipped fragments of glass or ceramics, mosaics incorporate what otherwise might be regarded as waste materials. Used simply, mosaics can make a patchwork effect, but in the hands of a patient master, they can form astonishing patterns.

Small tiles can be used, but for the serious recycler, fragments of pottery or glass make excellent mosaic materials. These will need to be firmly adhered to a solid backing board before being grouted and polished. This task is not to be taken lightly; if you are considering a mosaic, start with a small surface, such as a tabletop, before launching into larger projects. Although laborious, creating a mosaic surface is a satisfying task. Envisage the end result and persevere – it is worth the wait.

ECO FABRICS

CONSIDER AN INTERIOR AS A
SERIES OF LAYERS, BEGINNING
WITH HARD, DURABLE SURFACES
SUCH AS FLOORS AND WALLS,
MOVING ON THROUGH FURNITURE
AND FINISHING WITH FABRICS AND
SOFT FURNISHINGS. IT IS THE
CAREFUL CONSIDERATION OF ALL
OF THESE LAYERS THAT MAKES A
WELL-BALANCED AND ECO-
CONSCIOUS HOME.

As a tactile, decorative and insulating layer, fabrics play an important role in every interior. As well as adding colour, pattern and texture, fabrics can also reduce heat loss from a room when used to cover windows.

However, it is important to remember that the production of fabrics makes an enormous environmental impact; the quantities of chemicals, including insecticides and pesticides, used in the manufacture of even 'natural' materials, such as cotton, not to mention the water consumed, are quite staggering. What is more, many fabrics will have been exposed to further toxins, such as fire retardants, and perhaps coated in stain inhibitors. If this is the case, fabrics can bring toxins directly into your home, creating an unintended level of internal pollution within your living space.

OPPOSITE Eco fabrics can bring a richness to any interior using (clockwise from top left) cushions made from recycled seat belts, a natural wool felt rug, recycled vintage cottons, organic linen, an organic wool throw and an organic alpaca cushion.

The environmental impact of certain fabrics – for example, wool – can be lower than others. Likewise, as technology progresses, alternative manufacturing processes are being developed that will allow traditional fabrics to be created in more eco-friendly ways.

● FELT

For thousands of years, felt has been produced using one of the simplest manufacturing processes – one that can even be practised on a small scale at home. Felt is a non-woven textile that relies on the small scales of wool fibres (which expand when wet) to bind it together. Although it can be made using reclaimed fabric, historically felt is made using pure wool, and so its properties and colours can reflect the breed from which it was cut – some being hairier and coarser, while others, such as those made from merino, are softer. Generally felt is made by wetting and then compressing the wool, but it can also be heated with steam to help the fibres swell and interlock.

Being made from wool, felt is a sustainable material that is inherently biodegradable. It is also breathable and, due to its density, extremely warm, while retaining all of the characteristics of wool, including stain resistance and flame retardancy. It is a great material to work with, as it does not fray when cut, does not crease too readily and has good insulation qualities. So it works well when used as a flat-panel window covering. I love the visual weight and density of felt, which can be useful in absorbing noise in echoey rooms.

● INGEO™ POLYMERS

Ingeo™ is made using an annually replenishable base material, such as corn, which is processed to produce sugar from the plant starches. This sugar is then fermented to produce a high-performance polymer, from which Ingeo™ is extruded. With a natural material as its base, Ingeo™ is itself totally biodegradable under the right conditions.

Ingeo™ was invented some years ago but had previously been considered too expensive to produce in oil-rich countries, compared to petroleum-based fabrics such as nylon. As the price of oil has risen – making fabrics such as nylon more expensive – so fibres and materials with a natural base have once more become economically viable. As a processed fabric, Ingeo™ has a higher embodied energy than a fully natural one, but less so than a petrochemical-based fabric.

There are also eco concerns over the use of land for growing crops for textiles, rather than for food.

As a fabric, Ingeo™ has a variety of different forms and uses. Its benefits include being stain resistant, having low flammability, excellent UV stability, moisture management and low odour retention, and it is hypoallergenic. Its fibres can be made in different thicknesses, and so it is possible to make it into a variety of different products from bed linen, throws and pillows to upholstery, carpet, wall coverings and curtains.

● LYOCELL™

Lyocell™ is a man-made fibre created from the natural cellulose found in wood, which makes it a sustainable and 100% biodegradable material. Lyocell™ is made by first dissolving recycled paper with a solvent; the product is then recovered and recycled. The solvent breaks down the fibres of the paper, which are then reformed as it is passed through a series of tiny holes to create a thread.

Lyocell™ fabric is very strong (more so than cotton) and does not shrink or stretch; however, it does not take colour well, so dyes do have to be stronger. It also has a tendency to pill or bobble after time – but, since it is made of recycled paper, you should not be too hard on it.

In the near future, Lyocell™ may take the place of viscose and polyester (both petrochemical-based fabrics) and possibly even cotton, which uses vast quantities of land, water and chemicals to produce. Lyocell™ is currently used for clothing, bed linen, pillows and quilts.

OPPOSITE This careful arrangement of vintage fabric cushions brings an element of playfulness to a pure white interior space. This final layer of vintage creates a homely balance with the technological and natural elements of the living room.

ORGANIC COTTON

Cotton is one of the world's most ubiquitous materials, used in everything from clothes to curtains, towels to bed linens. It is made from the soft cellulose fibre that contains the seeds of the cotton plant; the seeds are removed and the fibres spun into a thread to make textiles. Cotton accounts for around 5% of all the cultivated land in the world, but the problem with conventional cotton production is that it also accounts for 25% of the world's pesticide usage. Because it is not an edible crop, much stronger chemicals are used to protect the valuable cotton from predators. This results in a whole host of contamination issues for the local flora and fauna, as well as for those workers who tend the crops.

By comparison, the increasingly wider cropping of organic cotton has combated many of the issues surrounding conventional production. Organic fertilisers are used, while natural pest management has reduced the need for pesticides. To protect those working in cotton production, fairtrade methods have been set up and are carefully monitored from the plant's growth through the fabric's production. This ensures that farmers (many of whom live in developing countries in vulnerable positions at the bottom of the supply chain) are paid a fixed fee – or market price if that is higher – and so guarantees them better standards of living and working conditions.

Organic cotton is now being used to produce a range of products, from clothes to tea towels and even bed linen. So if you are thinking about using cotton products, ensure that they are made from fairtrade organic cotton. Whilst it may be a little more expensive, you will have the assurance that neither the environment nor the lives of those producing it have been compromised.

ABOVE Flowing fine linen curtains add a romantic quality to this bedroom. The fabric filters the soft natural light, whilst offering an element of privacy.

ORGANIC WOOL

Few of us realise the fundamental importance of using organic wool for the health of both ourselves and the environment. Organic-wool sheep are reared on land free from potentially toxic chemicals, such as pesticides, and are never dipped; instead, they are bred to be naturally resistant to parasites. Once sheared, the wool (which can be greasy with lanolin) is scoured with biodegradable cleansers, before being carded and spun in a mill – the whole time being kept separate from 'contaminated' wool. To further avoid chemicals, heavy metals and processes, organic-wool products are often used undyed, ranging from natural creams to greys, browns and black. This not only keeps the wool toxin free but extends this benefit to the land, air, water and those who work in the industry; the impact really is huge.

There are 8,000 known chemicals in use within the textile industry; choosing organic wool will help to keep your home free from many of these. Often those thought to be allergic to wool are instead suffering reactions to the chemicals used to treat it, rather than to the wool itself.

Elsewhere in the home, wool's natural insulation and fire-retardant properties make it ideal for use as loft insulation. Because wool is breathable and can hold water, it acts not only to keep your home insulated (even when damp) but also to keep it cool in the heat; as the temperature outside rises, moisture evaporates, so drawing heat from the building and cooling it. Wool loft insulation costs a little more; but for my own home, I prefer to be able to venture up into the attic space without getting covered in those tiny shards that come off glass-fibre insulation.

ALPACA

The fibre of the alpaca is amazingly warm and luxurious, but also stronger and lighter than wool. Alpaca has a velvety softness; its hollow fibres make it very warm, and so it is perfect for weaving into blankets or throws.

Similar to llamas, although a little smaller, alpacas are hand reared, largely in South America – Peru, Chile and Bolivia – by smallholding farmers who shear and sell their fleece. There are very few of these animals: alpacas are not farmed intensively, which makes their fibre a sustainable product. Although this labour-intensive form of rearing makes alpaca fibre more costly, it does mean it is less vulnerable to heavily mechanised or chemical production methods, creating a lower embodied energy and a smaller environmental impact. As alpaca does not contain lanolin, it need not be scoured with chemical cleaning agents and so can be more gently processed. Unlike most other textile products, its embodied energy is related mostly to transportation, rather than manufacture.

Due to the variety of natural alpaca colours – there are up to 22 different shades, from creams to browns, greys to blacks, and even rose – it is less likely to be dyed when being made into products, so reducing its impact further.

LINEN

Made from flax, linen is highly sustainable since the whole plant can be used. Whilst the finer plant fibres are put to making linen, other parts are used to make linseed oil, livestock feed and even bank notes – so waste is minimised. Once cut and separated from the woody parts of the plant, the long, fine fibres are spun into a yarn and then woven into linen. Known as retting, this processing can be carried out naturally or be done chemically, which produces detrimental environmental byproducts. When buying linen, ask how it has been manufactured.

As linen is breathable it adjusts easily to body temperature, making it a good material for humid conditions – perfect for summer bed clothes. It also has a neutral pH, so is good for those who suffer from sensitive skin or conditions such as eczema. Linen's high absorbency makes it ideal for towels, tablecloths and bed linens. It is easily washed at low temperatures – good for energy saving – and softens with age but without pilling or bobbling. It does, however, have poor elasticity. This makes it crease easily; I think this just adds to the fabric's character, but it does make it a little more labour intensive to use.

HEMP

Hemp is set for a major comeback, due to its many environmental benefits. Industrial varieties are being grown with zero-THC content (tetrahydrocannabinol – the illegal drug bit or active chemical in cannabis), kickstarting its production on a wider scale.

As with linen, the entire hemp plant can be put to use. It is used to create foodstuffs, fabrics, papers, bodycare products, insulation and oil. Hemp grows in plantations with very little or no need for the use of pesticides and is very fast growing, soaking up a relatively high level of CO_2 and so reducing its environmental impact. For textiles, the stalk is cut, milled and then turned into yarn.

Hemp is a breathable fabric, and although it is often sold in naturally muted colours, its porous fibres easily take dyes. Hemp fabric can soften with use but remains hardwearing and of high tensile strength. It has good resistance to mould, strong UV protection and is naturally fire retardant.

Hemp is commonly used instead of cotton in clothing, carpets, insulation materials and much more. As a fabric it is coarser than cotton in its raw form – similar to linen in appearance – but now a number of designers are mixing it with other fibres, such as silk, to produce high-end fabrics. Extracting the fibres is labour intensive, which makes hemp time consuming and uneconomic to produce in many developed countries, but feasible in Eastern Europe and China where people power is still in force. However, there is a lot of research being carried out to find ways to change this, so watch this space.

PEACE SILK

Conventional silk is made by boiling the whole sillk worm cocoon, with the worm still alive inside, then unwinding the silk thread as whole strands onto reels. Only a few moths are released to breed in order to continue the population. Peace silk, however, is made by allowing the worms to emerge from their cocoons as moths, so living out their natural lifecycle. The cocoon is then degummed and spun like conventional fibres, rather than unreeled as one long thread, as it is damaged when the moth emerges. The resulting fabric has slightly different qualities to conventional silk but is purportedly warmer and softer.

RECYCLED TEXTILES

Reusing fabric is beneficial in a number of ways. It increases the lifespan of a fabric, reduces its embodied energy, minimises landfill and can help you to lower the level of toxins in your home. On top of all that, it means you will not be buying new man-made fabrics and will thereby be lowering the demand for pesticides, fire retardants and other chemicals used in the textile industry. And by eschewing high-energy manufacturing methods you can avoid increasing your carbon footprint.

You can find reclaimed fabrics in a variety of locations, including markets and antique stores, charity shops and online auction sites. Whilst you may not be able to find exactly what you want, it can open up a whole new creative design process – as long as you are open to the possibilities of what 'textile tapestries' can do for your home – by complementing or contrasting in pattern and colour. Using vintage fabrics can add richness to an interior scheme, often setting up an exciting contrast with other, more contemporary, features.

Whilst you could always use the fabrics as you find them – stitching pieces together can create wonderful patchwork curtains, cushions, covers for chairs and even clothes – if the colours are not right, you could always dye them to match your interior scheme. There is a real art to creating the perfect patchwork, and it helps to have a good eye for colour and texture.

As many vintage fabrics were produced before the introduction of fire retardants, or they may have off-gassed already, there is less chance that you will be bringing toxins into the home. That said, you may want to have vintage fabrics properly cleaned before using them.

ABOVE Crisp white bed linen combined with retro accessories and a vintage patchwork bedspread lend a familiar, nostalgic feel to this roof-level bedroom.

LEFT Without feeling cloying, the combination of vintage fabrics and patterned knits creates a sense of fun and lends character to this bedroom.

ECO LIGHTING

GOOD LIGHTING IS ESSENTIAL IF A HOME IS TO HAVE THE FLEXIBILITY DEMANDED BY CONTEMPORARY LIVING. ADEQUATE ILLUMINATION MAKES A HOME SAFE AND EASY TO USE, SATISFYING TO WORK IN, AND INVIGORATING. BY CONTRAST, IT CAN ALSO HELP A SPACE TO BE RELAXING OR EVEN ROMANTIC AFTER A LONG DAY AT WORK.

Having said that, we all need to reduce our carbon footprints by lowering our energy usage – and lighting is a significant area where cutbacks can be simply made. Considering that lighting accounts for on average 15% of the energy we consume in our homes, this is an important area to tackle.

First and foremost, we need to maximise our use of natural light in every area of the home. This can be done through a combination of three actions: allowing as much natural light into a space as possible (without leading to overheating), using reflective surfaces to bounce light around, choosing the right colour scheme to throw light back into your space.

But when the sun goes down and the artificial lights must go on, it is essential that the lighting you do have be practical yet uses as little energy as possible. Low-energy lighting products are being developed at a phenomenal rate, so gone are the days when you had to compromise on your lighting plan to reduce your energy usage. With the new types of lighting now available, ingenuity and imagination are still needed to create the perfectly lit, low environmental impact space.

OPPOSITE Low-energy lighting need never be dull; just exercise a little imagination (clockwise from top left): portable rechargable eco lights, a recycled vintage glass chandelier, a low-energy bulb in a design-classic anglepoise lamp, a reclaimed jelly mould transformed into a lampshade, low-energy fairylights attached to branches and natural wool felt lampshades that stay cool next to energy-saving lightbulbs.

COMPACT FLUORESCENT LIGHTBULBS

Compact fluorescent lightbulbs (CFLs) are currently the easiest way for us all to reduce our carbon footprint with little hassle or cost. They last up to ten times longer than conventional lightbulbs and over that lifespan use around 80% less energy. In fact that is up to 10,000 hours instead of 1,000 hours and around 15 watts instead of an equivalent 60 watts of energy. Bearing in mind that the average household has around 22 lights, if every lightbulb were changed from tungstens to CFLs, this would add up to a massive saving in both energy use and carbon emissions, not to mention financial savings for you.

However, CFLs do have a few associated issues. They take a little time to reach their optimum brightness; so they are not ideal for use in a hallway, for example, where your need for light may have passed by the time they are fully functioning. Added to which, CFLs do not like to be turned on and off frequently, so they cannot be used with some automatic timer switches. When CFLs finally expire, they must be disposed of properly since each bulb contains a small amount of mercury (imagine a pellet smaller than the end of a biro), which can be recovered. If the mercury goes into landfill, there is a possibility that it might contaminate, but many local authorities are not yet set up to deal with this recycling issue.

Technology in this area is moving fast and CFLs are consistently being improved. They are now available in different shades – soft white generally works best for homes – and their elements are being encased in rubber-coated frosted glass, so they are beginning to look more like conventional tungsten lightbulbs. Furthermore, CFLs can now even be dimmed, which makes them more flexible. CFLs are available in a selection of shapes and sizes to suit every light fitting – from the conventional bulb shape to candle bulbs, pygmy bulbs and now even as substitutes for halogen spotlights, known as GU10s.

If you are averse to the appearance of CFLs, but feel you ought to use them, conceal the bulb with a large lampshade – perhaps one made of felt or paper, since they emit so little heat. Or use a number of small ones in an intricate chandelier.

LIGHT EMITTING DIODES

Light emitting diodes (LEDs) are set to become the lighting of the future as tungsten bulbs and then energy saving bulbs are eventually phased out. In fact, you may already be using them if you own a set of new bike lights. LEDs are incredibly efficient, lasting for up to 50,000 hours and using a fraction of the energy of other bulbs (at just 2 to 3 watts), while producing very little heat. In fact, their life span is actually even longer than this, though after this time their brightness will start to dim.

LEDs are available in a wide variety of sizes and shapes, so can replace traditional bulbs, spotlights and even fluorescent tubes. In addition they can be specified as dimmable or colour changing for ultimate lighting flexibility and creating atmosphere within the home. Cheaper, more common bulbs are found as a bright (but cold) white; so ensure you specify warm white for the home. LEDs are predominantly used in the form of small spotlights, so are best employed as replacements for halogen bulbs, as general or more focused task lighting.

When specifying LED lighting, speak to an expert who can guide you in choosing the correct bulbs, fittings, drivers (which act like transformers), switches and switch plates as the lighting industry is slow to keep pace with this developing product.

HALOGENS

Within these lights, electricity is passed through a filament, which is surrounded by halogen gas. Similar to traditional lightbulbs, halogens produce a lot of heat; this is inefficient, as it is energy that could otherwise be converted into light. It is also a frequent misconception that low voltage means low energy – it does not. Halogens simply run on different voltages and so need transformers. In fact, halogens have a lifespan of around 4,000 hours but still use twice the energy of CFLs and considerably more than their LED equivalents (though energy saving versions are now available with 30% less energy use).

Originally intended as spotlights, halogens are now used for general lighting and liberally perforate ceilings, especially in bathrooms and

ABOVE Colour-changing LEDs can be used to create atmosphere. However, they are best used in a subtle manner, within a small palette of shades to match your interior scheme.

RIGHT Vintage lighting can discretely conceal low-energy lightbulbs. This cool combination of romantic crystal chandelier and retro chrome side light creates a functional but irreverent feel to the space.

kitchens. In my opinion, the quality of light produced by halogens is harsh and full of glare. Halogens are also expensive and as they do need changing fairly frequently so they tend to be an expensive way to light a space.

However, it is not all bad news. If your home is full of halogen light fittings the bulbs can be refitted with CFL or, even better, LED replacements, leading to massive savings in energy and cost – not to mention ladder time.

● FLUORESCENT TUBES

Despite their poor reputation gained through their association with soulless office spaces, fluorescent tube lights perform well in providing an even spread of light across a surface, emitting around four times more light for the energy they consume than conventional tungsten lightbulbs. Fluorescent tube lights work in a similar way to CFLs – electricity runs through a gas to create light. Fluorescent tubes do not produce much heat, instead converting most of the electricity used into light, so are very efficient and can last for between 10,000 and 20,000 hours. They are available in different colours, allowing you to use warmer tones in the home than might be appropriate within a commercial space.

The trick with fluorescent tubes is to conceal them – this will cut down on any aggravating glare and ensure that the tube cannot be seen at all, just the glow of reflected light. This can be done by running them along the top of eye-level units in the kitchen or across the top of fitted cupboards in bedrooms to bounce light off a white ceiling. I love to experiment with these lights; the results can be surprising and give a space a real glow.

Once your fluorescent tube has blown or broken, it must be properly disposed of. This can be done either through your local authority or via certain electrical retailers.

✿ CANDLES

There are inherent dangers in using candles, but when carefully managed and not left unattended, they produce a beautiful, romantic form of light. Candlelight has a soft, warm glow, a gentle charismatic flicker and, when positioned on a table at eye level in a candelabrum, they light faces evenly with no harsh shadows.

Even candles have an environmental impact, however, so it is worth knowing that some candles are more eco-friendly than others. Conventional paraffin wax candles are most common and easy to buy but they release a black smoke and soot when burnt. This soot, which will blacken ceilings, walls and fabrics over time, actually contains eleven known toxins of which two are carcinogenic (toluene and benzene).

The alternatives to paraffin wax candles are palm wax or soy candles, which are cleaner and whiter burning. Palm wax is derived from the fruit of the palm oil tree, which is grown in tropical areas and is used largely in foods, toiletries and cosmetics. It is important to check that the palm oil comes from a well-managed, sustainable source, which will not contribute to the destruction of tropical rainforests, wildlife habitats or communities; the governing body of which is the Roundtable on Sustainable Palm Oil (RSPO).

Equally, when buying soy oil candles it is important to ensure they are made with 100% natural ingredients and essential oils, not from a GM source of soy or topped up with man-made chemicals or fragrances. And why not try making your own? I love using vintage bone china tea cups filled with natural soy wax and scented candle oils. The soft, flickering light glows beautifully through the translucent sides of the cup, creating a little table top magic.

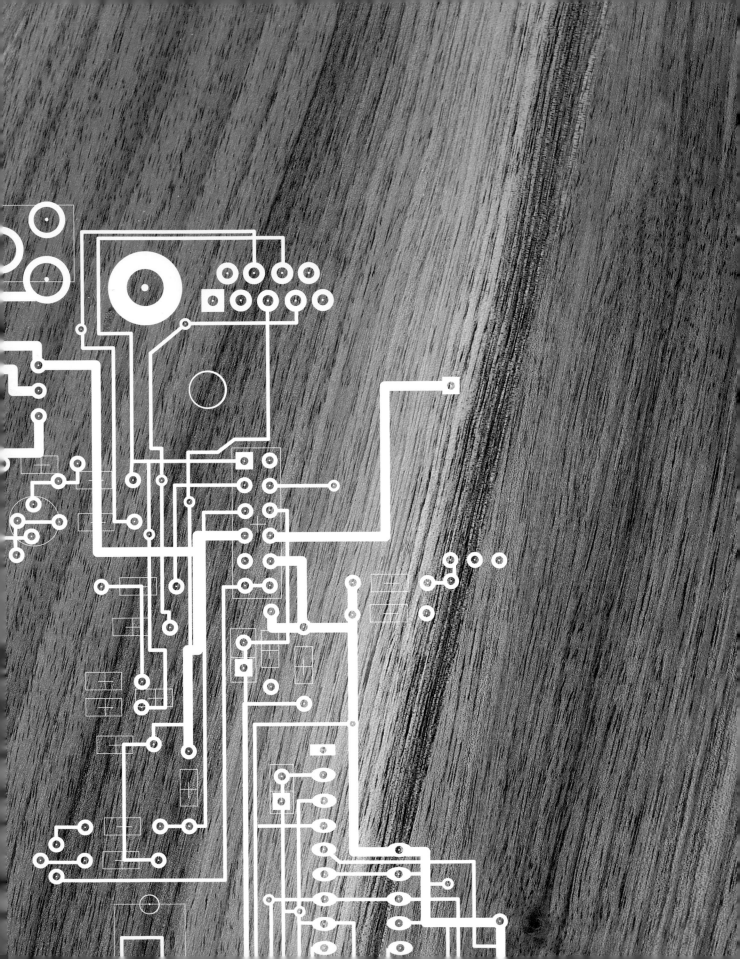

IN THE HOME

KITCHENS AND DINING ROOMS

IT IS WITHIN THE KITCHEN THAT WE USE THE MOST RESOURCES – A HIGH PROPORTION OF THE WATER, ELECTRICITY AND GAS WE CONSUME ARE FED INTO THIS SPACE. BE LESS WASTEFUL AND ENSURE THAT EVERY LITRE, WATT AND CUBIC METRE ARE USED IN THE MOST EFFICIENT WAY POSSIBLE.

Similarly, a large proportion of the packaging and food we consume on a daily basis finds its way into the kitchen, so the opportunity to recycle and compost is also present. Anyone who is serious about cutting their carbon footprint must focus their eco thoughts on the kitchen.

When thinking about your kitchen, consider the impact of its entire lifecycle – from how it is manufactured, through its everyday use, to what will happen to it once it has reached the end of its useful life. On top of these practical concerns, the kitchen is a major investment so it should also be durable, cost effective and ultimately a selling point for your home. In short, the design of the perfect eco kitchen has to fulfil all of these criteria not forgetting that it is the heart of the home, so it needs to be a welcoming and a pleasurable space to be in.

ECO KITCHEN PLANNING

Planning an environmentally friendly kitchen is much like planning a conventional kitchen, except to be truly eco a kitchen must be built from materials chosen from a specific eco-friendly palette, all appliances must be A-rated energy efficient goods and within the

ABOVE A decidely vintage kitchen. Rather than being wastefully ripped out, these retro units have been given a new lease of life with a coat of warm cream paint. The homely feel that such vintage units lend a kitchen is accentuated by the casual arrangements of personal objects.

layout adequate space for waste recycling must be incorporated. Obviously, maximising available space, light and creating an efficient layout will make your kitchen lower impact and easier to use, thereby giving it a longer life span, but in the kitchen it is also important to remember the green mantra of the 3Rs: reduce, reuse and recycle (see pages 14–16).

When planning an urban eco chic kitchen, you will want to focus on anything that allows you to reduce the amount of resources the kitchen needs in both its construction and in its daily use. Look for ways to cut water, electricity and gas usage – you will reap the rewards in time. Likewise, if you can reuse old items or use sustainably produced materials in your design it will help you to cut the environmental footprint of your kitchen. Ask yourself whether you really need to rip out the entire existing kitchen to fit a new one or could you simply replace certain elements to give it a whole new feel? If so, you could look to replace only the worksurfaces, splashbacks and door handles whilst covering or painting the old doors – it really can make a dramatic difference.

Using naturally produced materials will help to cut the level of toxins present. From a personal health perspective, the kitchen is a place of food preparation so it makes sense to cut down on the use of toxic materials and those that off-gas over longer periods of time within this space.

Whilst recycling kitchen waste is something we are all now familiar with, it rests at the bottom of the 3Rs hierarchy as ideally you will cut down on what is thrown away in the first place. But also look to use recycled materials in your kitchen's construction and allow adequate space for recycling packaging and foodstuffs within its design. As recycling processes improve and it is possible to recycle more and more materials, so we will need additional storage space in our kitchens – future-proof your home now.

TECHNOLOGY, NATURE AND VINTAGE

The cornerstones of urban eco chic come into their own in the kitchen; a space that combines high resources usage, functionality and style. Technology provides beautiful cutting-edge low-impact materials that can be incorporated into a room and allows appliances to cut down on the amount of resources needed to fuel a kitchen – from dishwashers that use less water than washing-up by hand through to low-energy lights that will last for years and can even be programmed to change colour.

The inclusion of nature can create exciting textural contrasts between surfaces and appliances within a kitchen. As well as reducing the level of toxins present, natural materials, such as timber, often improve with age, picking up a rich patina with prolonged usage. Natural materials are also easier to recycle at the end of their life as they can simply biodegrade.

Incorporating vintage items in the kitchen may add a sense of character to a space that can all too easily be shiny, pristine and soulless. Whether it is a collection of mismatched chairs, an aged sideboard or an antique glass-fronted display cabinet, vintage pieces provide warmth and comfort within a home.

FAR LEFT Sometimes furniture that was not originally intended for a kitchen can make ideal storage. This old library catalogue unit with its plentiful compartments is a great piece for a vintage kitchen.

LEFT Natural wood does not always have to look rustic. When carefully machined and highly sanded, wood can take on a very polished look. Here the quality is all in the detail and the exquisitely crafted dovetail joints on each drawer.

OPPOSITE This attic apartment kitchen successfully blends technology – the machined stainless steel units and efficient modern appliances – and nature – the rough oak beams and blockwood worksurfaces – with a smattering of vintage pieces, such as the plan chest and kitchen chairs.

KITCHEN CARCASSES

The carcasses of kitchen units are mostly made from recycled woodchips, bonded together with a formaldehyde or polyurethane resin to form chipboard, which is then covered with a melamine surface finish. In eco terms, this can be both good and bad: on the one hand there is a high recycled content in these boards, which is good, but if they contain fomaldehyde they may off-gas toxins, which is bad. Sadly, chipboard carcasses are not very durable – incredibly, chipboard is not waterproof, so if you have a leaky tap or a flood your cabinets can be ruined – so they have only a limited lifespan and are difficult to recycle at the end of their useful life. Whenever possible, it makes sense to reuse old chipboard carcasses that may no longer off-gas toxins. Alternatively, use cabinets made up of a solid board material such as ZF-MDF (zero formaldehyde medium density fibreboard), which will not off-gas formaldehyde toxins.

KITCHEN CABINET DOORS

As a vertical plane, doors play a significant part in the look of your kitchen units. Use them to inject colour, a sense of nature or period style. Whatever you do, make sure they have no adverse effect on your health or the environment.

From a functional point of view, the material should be easy to clean, resistant to scratches, and sufficiently strong to allow for proper fixing. When fixing hinges to doors, ensure the material is at least 18mm thick, or adhere it to a substrate board, such as ZF-MDF, to make it up to this.

There are a number of materials for cabinet doors; the technology option will create a sleek contemporary finish, the nature option will add a feeling of natural warmth and texture and, whilst it may require more work, the vintage option is likely to be the cheapest of the three and have a more characterful feel.

TECHNOLOGY

◉ ZF-MDF panels – these can be cut, routed, and painted with a foam roller, much like conventional MDF.

◉ Recycled plastic sheets – these come in an array of colours and styles so choose one that will complement the rest of your kitchen.

◉ Multi-application recycled plastic sheeting – these are created from recycled detergent bottles, mobile phones and even wellington boots; use the sleek whites or slick blacks, but stay away from the multi-coloured panels.

◉ Melamine-faced chipboards – although bonded by resin glues with the potential to off-gas toxins, these boards can be made of up to 70% post-consumer woodchips from pallets and fruit crates, so they have a recycled content of materials that otherwise end up in landfill. However, once damaged they cannot be repaired so have a lower durability rating.

NATURE

🍃 Solid timber panels – fixed to a substrate board, these can be vertical or horizontal strips to give a sense of layering, visually increasing the length or height of the space.

🍃 Plywood panels – fixed onto sliding rails, the front face of the plywood may be veneered with a thin layer of another type of timber or alternatively left natural or stained with a wood dye.

VINTAGE

❀ Reclaimed timber – these timbers, including wire-brushed or painted floorboards, can be made into panel doors.

❀ Fabric hanging panels – fixed onto a cable, these panels can be slid from side to side.

❀ Old sail fabric – fixed onto a hook system, this fabric can look great if sewn carefully so the nautical numbers and symbols show.

KITCHEN SINKS

Any trip to a reclamation yard acts as a reminder that a kitchen is rarely for life. Many kitchens have a lifespan of only 10–12 years. It is worth remembering this when choosing fixtures and fittings, including sinks. Some materials, such as Durat® recycled plastics, can have sinks seamlessly welded to the worksurface creating a sleek professional look (see page 72). This can be in the same colour as the worksurface or a contrasting hue for variation; either way it is a good water-tight design method.

Stainless steel sinks are available in a wide variety of shapes, sizes and costs. The material is enormously durable and easy to maintain with the added benefit that stainless steel is easy to recycle, so your sink is likely to already contain a percentage of recycled material. If you have a solid core worksurface, such as timber, choose an under-mounted style sink that fixes to the underside of the worksurface for a sleeker finish. It is also easier to use with no surface edges to catch dirt, crumbs or prevent water from draining back into the sink. Salvage yards may also have a selection of disused commercial stainless steel kitchen units with integral sinks – perfect if you aspire to being the 'pro' chef of the household.

Alternatively, opt for a traditional fireclay (ceramic) sink. Whilst they have a high initial embodied energy usage due to the firing process, they are durable, long lasting and easy to maintain. Visit your local reclamation yard to seek out heritage-style fireclay sinks, which are perenially popular. They will bring a rustic farmhouse quality to your kitchen with their simple, practical aesthetic.

KITCHEN TAPS

The water flow from a running tap at standard mains pressure can be upwards of 10–12 litres per minute; ideally this ought to be reduced to around six litres per minute. A reduction in water usage may be achieved by simply consuming less in the first place – for example, cleaning dishes or vegetables in a washing-up bowl rather than in the sink, saving precious litres every day – but if you are fitting new taps choose water-efficient, low-flow models. Do bear in mind that a water flow rate of any less than six litres per minute feels frustratingly slow when filling a pan or bucket. When selecting a tap be sure to check that your choice works at the water pressure flowing to your home – measured in bars, often a minimum water pressure of 0.5 bar is required.

For water-aware options consider the following:
- Fit a monobloc single tap – this reduces material usage (as you require only the one tap) and mixes the hot and cold water instantly to the required temperature.
- Turn down the flow valves that lead from the water pipes to the taps – a simple adjustment is all that is needed, but ensure enough water still flows to activate your boiler for hot water. This restricts water usage in a crude way, but will not regulate the flow rate.
- Fit a conventional monobloc tap with flow regulators fitted into the pipes (both the hot and cold) below the tap as low-flow taps are not always the most attractive. This keeps the flow at a steady rate of 4–6 litres per minute.
- Fit a monobloc tap with a cartridge that has two flow levels – the first level for a general low-flow rate, but then push the lever further to the second level for a faster flow rate.

ABOVE There is no reason why you cannot choose the taps you really want, as long as they are fitted with flow restrictors or aerators to reduce water usage. This spring-mounted, commercial-style plate washer tap provides a functional contrast to the natural wood cladding and stacks of cream crockery.

LEFT Mixer taps are a good choice for an eco kitchen. As they blend the hot and cold together, you can control the water temperature at source and reduce wastage.

○ Fit a tap with an aerating head – this gives the impression of a faster flow rate whilst delivering only six litres per minute. On some conventional taps with a threaded end a simple aerator can be screwed in, but check sizes and dimensions before buying.

❀ Visit your local reclamation yard to seek out the vintage option – taps are often thrown out in full working condition when a new kitchen is fitted. If they need work, they may just require new washers and re-chroming. Vintage taps do not have a high resale value so this can make for a good budget option too. Fit vintage taps with flow regulators for the ultimate in urban eco chic style.

ADDITIONAL TAPS

In the kitchen you may also want to consider a filtered drinking water tap, which removes any impurities from mains water. This will cut down on the amount of plastic drinking water bottles that you have to recycle as it will provide you with a continuous supply of fresh filtered water for both cooking and drinking. Some taps have a built-in tri-flow system allowing an extra built-in tap to take water from a carbon filter system and straight through the conventional spout. If you are worried about any cross-contamination, however, use a separate tap and spout system.

A more recent development in taps – and one that is set to become a feature in many kitchens – is the instant-boil tap. One press of the lever and straightaway the water boils through air pressure alone as opposed to a conventional heating element. This dramatically cuts down on the energy used to boil water as well as the amount of hot water used; it is easy enough to put the water straight into the cup or pan that you are using with no wasteful surplus.

SPLASHBACKS

Splashbacks are the vertical areas that sit to the rear of your worksurfaces, so they have a significant impact on the look of your kitchen. Whilst they need not be quite as hardwearing as the worksurfaces themselves, their primary function is to act as easy-to-clean surfaces that prevent liquids from dribbling down the back of the kitchen cabinets, which can in time lead to the growth of unhealthy mould.

The splashback provides a visual opportunity to add exciting textural detail to your kitchen; but remember that keeping surfaces light and reflective will help to bounce natural light around the space. This vertical plane is highly visible and separates the eye-level cabinets from the worksurface. So be careful not to use too many materials in your kitchen's palette – it can lead to a messy, uncoordinated feel.

For suitable splashback options, consider any of the following:
● Ecoresin™ panels – there is a great variety of these ecoresin panels to choose from, clear, coloured or even incorporating other decorative materials, such as flowers or reeds, encased within them (see page 66). Furthermore, these resin panels are easy to work with even when the specified measurements are not quite correct. They can look quite spectacular.
● Extended worksurfaces – match the material of the splashback to your worksurface. Whether it is timber, bamboo or slate, consider extending the kitchen worksurface vertically up the wall by 10–20cm. This will keep your kitchen coordinated and unfussy. Paint the surface above the splashback to match the rest of the kitchen.

● Painted walls – use a VOC-free eggshell or emulsion paint that contains no toxins as you do not want toxins drifting down onto your food preparation area (see page 65). Painted walls are not as hardwearing as other splashback materials, and you will need to fit a quadrant detail between the worksurface and the wall to fill the joint and to stop liquids, but it will simply co-ordinate the kitchen with no fuss.
● Back-painted glass – large sheets of glass can be ordered with any colour you choose. This can be easy to clean and maintain, giving a light-reflective, contemporary feel.
● Mosaic, glass or ceramic tiles – these are easy to fit, as you can avoid cutting, thereby reducing any unnecessary wastage (see page 75). Ideally source tiles made locally in the country where you live in order to avoid any excess transportation.
● Conventional ceramic or stone tiles – again try to source tiles that have not travelled vast distances (see page 75). These can be refreshed every few years by re-grouting them. Avoid using tile paints to refresh your kitchen, as they can have high toxic VOC contents, which will fall onto your food preparation areas.
● Stainless steel – easy to clean, light-reflective and professional looking (see page 72). It is often made from recycled materials and can itself be recycled. You must measure up carefully before ordering as there is no room to alter its shape once the steel arrives.
● Recycled glass tiles – these can be sourced in a variety of back-painted colours (as opposed to clear, which would allow you to see the wall behind) which gives them a translucent depth (see page 66). You can be creative with the colours (horizontal stripes work well), but try not to go overboard.

TIPS FOR **REDUCING** KITCHEN WASTE

● Do not accept plastic bags, buy a reusable shopping bag or bag for life and place it on a hook on the back of your front door, so it is always there when you go out shopping.

● If you do accept plastic bags, make sure you reuse them as often as possible.

● Use re-sealable storage boxes wherever possible instead of throwaway freezer bags.

● Reuse tin foil whenever you can.

● Buy fruit and vegetable loose rather than encased in any packaging – this is favoured by local greengrocers but less so by supermarkets.

● Recycle organic matter and cardboard in a home compost system.

● Grow as many of your own vegetables as you can.

● Choose products with packaging that can be recycled – those made with more than one material are difficult to separate. Market forces can help change the world.

● Do not buy heavily processed food in its own cooking dish with lots of unnecessary packaging.

● Find out what your local authority can recycle; you may be surprised by what they reprocess.

● Be creative rather than throw items away – for instance, use glass jars as nightlight candle holders in the garden.

KITCHEN RECYCLING

In an ideal world we would all do more to reduce the amount we buy and subsequently throw away. However, that is not always realistic, or indeed even wholly possible in our consumer world, so we need to incorporate proper facilities for recycling in every kitchen. Yes, recycling can be time consuming and a bit of a pain, but it is essentially very easy to do. So the best way forward is to embrace it as an essential part of modern-day life. It really will take only a small change in the attitude of us all to make a world of difference. If you need further convincing, visit your local landfill site.

Depending on how much you and your family consume, you may need to devote a surprising amount of space to recycling facilities within your kitchen. The pressure on kitchen space can be reduced by finding alternative storage areas, such as an understairs cavity or a hallway cupboard, for items before they are collected and taken to recycling facilities.

It is likely you will want to and be able to recycle: **GLASS • TIN CANS • DRINKS CANS • PAPER • PHONE DIRECTORIES • CARDBOARD • BATTERIES • SOME PLASTIC CONTAINERS • ORGANIC WASTE**

Many of these recyclable items can be unsightly and so storage for them is often best hidden away. This could be the cupboard area underneath the sink but, due to the bulk of the sink itself as well as the u-tubes, often this space is often not big enough to store all the necessary items or even to position a compartmentalised recycling bin. You may need to find an alternative cupboard or to use a separate dedicated recycling bin.

RECYCLING STORAGE

There are a number of neat folding, sliding and swing-open compartmentalised recycling bins on the market, which help you sort and store items prior to recycling. Choose whichever one is best suited to your needs and available space. Measure your cupboard and check the bin opens sufficiently for you to access every compartment. If there are any obstacles to hassle-free recycling, it easily cuts down the amount you and your family actually recycle. If you have no space in your cupboards, choose a free-standing separating bin. My own three-section compartment bin has a flip-up lid, which makes it easy to use even when your hands are full.

If you are finding that cans and bottles take up too much space, use a crusher – its long levers make light work of compressing items ready to be recycled. In addition, you may want to find a way to store all those plastic bags that you have promised yourself to stop collecting. They do really pile up, but can be neatly stored away for future reuse.

Recycling organic waste, such as vegetable peelings, eggshells and other food scraps, can be an unsightly and unpleasant experience. It is best to get any compostable matter right out of the way into a kitchen caddy with a removable lid, which can then be frequently emptied onto your compost heap or into your curbside collection bin. However, a neater alternative is to under-mount a removable organics bin beneath a hole cut in the kitchen worksurface, which is accessed via a neatly fitting lid. The flush surface-mounted fitting has a rubber seal that prevents smells escaping from beneath the lid. This makes it a neat, integrated and easy-to-use option, without creating extra clutter to sit on the kitchen worksurface.

There is still some debate about the usefulness of electric in-sink waste disposal units. Whilst they do reduce the amount of organic waste that is driven to landfill, they also use up quantities of water and electricity to grind waste matter into an unpleasant sludge that goes into the sewers, occassionally blocking them, before being ending up at a treatment plant and going to landfill. If possible, it is better for everyone to use a home compost system or curbside organic waste recycling system instead.

WALLS

It goes without saying that in a kitchen/dining space you will want to cut the levels of toxins as far as possible. Conventional paints off-gas VOCs over time (see page 65): these colourless gases are heavier than air and, as they fall onto kitchen worksurfaces, may attach themselves to food as it is being prepared. There is a real danger of ingesting these VOCs. Cut this out by using natural VOC-free paints or inert materials, such as ceramic tiles, in food preparation areas.

In a dining area you may want to create a different atmosphere from that in the kitchen. Paint kitchen walls in pale shades to bounce light around the space and keep it feeling fresh. By contrast, you can afford to be a little more adventurous in the dining area. Look to use darker shades of paint, wallpapers and hangings or drapes to create a mood. When both kitchen and dining areas are part of one open-plan space, juxtaposing finishes can work well to subtly zone areas of differing functions.

APPLIANCES

A kitchen is likely to house a number of expensive, energy-hungry electrical items some of which are difficult to do without. Fridges, freezers, cookers, hobs and now even dishwashers are considered by many to be totally indispensable. In recent years it has become easy enough to purchase energy- and resource-efficient machines thanks to clear Energy Efficiency labels. Whilst more efficient appliances may have a higher initial cost, it is important to consider the long-term impact after purchase. Buying higher quality items

means you can often expect them to be more durable and have a longer life. Being energy efficient means that they will cost you less to run over the entire period of their useful life. Energy ratings for white goods range from A to G, where A is the most efficient and G the least. However, a number of appliances have now surpassed this efficiency rating system so are available as A++, AA or even AAA.

Whilst buying the right energy-efficient item is a good place to start, there are some other basic rules to consider. When planning to purchase white goods of any type, do some homework first. Study the manufacturer's specifications and read online reviews by other users and consumer research groups to gain a real understanding of the product's construction, durability and efficiency. Lastly, remember the manufacture and transport of electrical items takes an enormous amount of energy and outputs a high level of toxins into the environment, placing an impact and embodied energy level onto any new appliance; buying better and less often is the best way forward.

FRIDGES AND FREEZERS

● Fridges and freezers stacked one above the other are up to 20% more efficient than separates that sit underneath worksurfaces.
● Never position a cold appliance, such as a fridge, next to a hot item, such as a dishwasher, as it will reduce their efficiency.
● A full freezer is more efficient so keep it stocked with food or even rolled-up newspaper.
● Make sure you dispose of your old fridge or freezer properly via your local authority.

COOKERS AND HOBS

● Whilst cooking with gas is considered more efficient, it is a limited carbon-heavy resource. Whereas electricity can, of course, come from a renewable energy source such as wind turbines or photovolatics (see pages 38–43).
● Cooking with an electric induction hob can be up to 74% efficient, compared to 43% for gas. Induction hobs heat just the base of the ferrous pan with little waste heat spilling out either side. They are also easy to clean and highly controllable, meaning that those who use electric induction hobs to cook, love them.

● Large-capacity ovens take a long time to heat up, drawing a lot of energy. If possible have two ovens, one large and one small – perfect for cooking for different numbers.
● A conventional oven is less efficient than a convection fan-assisted oven.
● An air extraction unit is a necessity to draw away fumes and smells and ventilate cooking areas. Look for energy-efficient models.
● A microwave uses less energy to cook food and in less time, but it can encourage the use of excessively packaged, processed ready meals as opposed to the eating of freshly prepared foods.
❀ Choose models made with stainless steel, which can be recycled at their lifecycle's end.

DISHWASHERS

● It is believed the most efficient dishwashers may use less water – some manufacturers say up to 80% less – to wash the equivalent number of dishes than when done by hand. But the machine must be full to capacity.
● Dishwashers are available in a variety of different sizes – standard, half-width and even pull-out drawer versions, so find the one that is right for the number of people in your home.
● If your dishwasher is located in a kitchen/dining space, noise pollution from the machine can be a real pain. Enquire how loud your chosen dishwasher is and compare it to other available models.
● Buy a dishwasher with a long guarantee (up to five years), which suggests the manufacturer is confident of the machine's durability.
● Some dishwashers can sense how dirty the dishes are (through testing the water during the cycle) and adjust the amount of energy and water used accordingly.

TABLES AND CHAIRS

Alongside beds and sofas, the dining table is one of the most significant home furnishings. In my mind, it is the social hub of the home around which all shared activity centres. When used regularly for meals, it is the one real chance we get to sit face-to-face to interact without distraction. It becomes a vital part of the daily, monthly and yearly routine – introducing an element of ritual into the lives of those who use it, which will be both grounding and orienting.

Choosing the right dining table is something that you should take time over, ensuring it is the right style, size and type for your home. You could opt for a straightforward fixed size and shape table, which will give a sense of stability and structure to the space. If you are pushed for room, a flip-up or fold-out table will still transform your home into a sociable space. Some retailers sell adjustable wall brackets that support a table for two or fold-out timber table and chair sets. Alternatively, if the number of people who may sit around the table is likely to vary or you are into dinner parties, look for an extending table. Introducing flexibility into any item of furniture means that you are making an environmental saving – you are effectively buying two tables with the impact of only one.

Similarly the chairs that you choose to go with the table will add to the whole impact of your dining area and can offer a chance to create something really exciting. Whilst many retailers sell matching table and chair sets, this can sometimes look very formal, creating a very set piece. Do not be afraid to mix up styles of chairs – add cohesiveness with small details such as soft fabric covers in one colour or material.

ABOVE A successful mix of vintage chairs can look less contrived than an entire set of one 'matchy-matchy' style. With vintage furniture becoming increasingly sought-after, why not start a collection of key pieces?

DINING TABLES

Remember the urban eco chic principles of technology, nature and vintage? Each will impact on the overall style of your dining space in varying ways, creating different looks. The technology options will create a slick, clean sophisticated feel in your dining space; the nature options will add a sense of wholesome, natural dining with a feeling of solidity and real warmth; alternatively the vintage pieces will add a quirkier more unusual characterful feeling to your space – real one-offs:

TECHNOLOGY

⦿ Glass tabletops with fixed or simple trestle table legs – these can allow light to filter through the tabletop to bounce off the floor and up into the room. Glass does have a high embodied energy through the manufacturing process but enjoys a classic, enduring style.

⦿ Recycled plastic tabletops mixed with new or vintage bases and legs – these are available in a number of speckled colours and make good surfaces. Some plastics can be overpowering, but those with simple or single shades work well to produce an easy-to-clean durable surface.

⦿ Recycled glass stone tabletops – crushed recycled glass makes for an exciting and sparkling surface (see page 72). It is warm to the touch and very smooth. You can choose the proportions of glass and background resin colour to tie in with the design of the rest of the space. This will be a real talking point.

⦿ Plywood tabletops – a number of manufacturers are now making cut-out plywood furniture that has a phenolised (dark brown colour) or melamine (often white) surface. This has the advantage of being transported as a flat plywood surface for much of its material life, both to the place of manufacture and to your home, making it an efficient and contemporary dining table solution. Other forms of natural plywood can be used, but the top surface can be relatively soft and prone to being easily scratched.

NATURE

🍂 Timber – a solid timber table will have a visual weight and earthy sense of wholesomeness. It will age well – improving over the years and mellowing in colour – acquiring an heirloom quality. Choose one made from FSC-certified timber (see page 57), ideally grown in your own country. Oak, pine, spruce or beech are good options. Being a solid surface, if scratched, timber can simply be sanded down to hide any marks. Finish with a Danish oil or natural wax to bring out the texture of the grain and warmth of the material.

🍂 Reclaimed teak – tables are being made from teak by a number of manufacturers and have a rich red colouration. The timber is reclaimed from buildings being torn down in the Far East and India, manufactured into furniture before being shipped. Remember that this furniture will have a higher carbon footprint than any made in your own country. Ensure that your supplier has FSC certifications and follows fairtrade practices.

🍂 Bamboo – this multi-functional material is tough and durable (see page 57). As it grows so fast, it is very reasonably priced. Like many timbers it has natural anti-bacterial properties, which makes it good for worksurfaces and tabletops. Again, this material is likely to have been manufactured in the Far East so will have a high carbon footprint.

ABOVE Recycled glass stone has been used here to create a diner-style kitchen table. Teamed with sleek plywood benches and contemporary plastic chairs, this kitchen scores high on eco-friendly technology.

VINTAGE

You do not have to look far to find a vintage timber table – markets, antique stores, junk shops, online auction sites are all great sources for furniture that has a ready-worn, rich patina. They can have a relaxed, distinctly unprecious quality, which can make them great for informal family dining. Clean them gently and simply re-oil the timber to retain its true character. Alternatively, you could find a retro glass-topped table that will add an air of character and style to your home. For real style, look for tables from the 1950s and '60s with chromed steel legs.

❀ Reclaimed timber – this can make for an exciting DIY project. Visit your local timber reclamation yard and find anything from old scaffold boards and floorboards to slices of real timber that still has the bark on the sides.
❀ Use your imagination and track down a really unusual piece – this could be as simple as an old door or even an industrial table. One of my own favourite tables was made from a reclaimed leather-cutting table, which I then suspended from the ceiling.
❀ Re-cover an old wooden table using mosaic tiles or fragments of pottery – this will create a unique but satisfying piece.

KITCHENWARES

If you have gone to the trouble of creating your very own eco kitchen and dining area, it is a shame to fill it with products that have neither the environmental credentials nor the style to match. Luckily, there is a vast array of beautifully eco chic kitchenware to choose from that has taken its impact into consideration, whether it is low-energy, fairtrade or from a sustainable or recycled source.

CROCKERY

It is important for crockery to be durable, so that it can be used over and over again, be put through a dishwasher or sluiced around the sink. At the same time, however, as it is an item that is used with such frequency, it is essential that it complements your table and your food. Luckily, there are several urban eco chic options:

◉ Recycled glass – made from crushed recycled bottles, this is often clear with a slight greenish tinge. It is often of high quality, very durable and, I am glad to say, also very stylish. It is available in a range of styles and sizes and in a number of colours – with a back-painted finish – that can be mixed and matched to add interest to your table. Being dishwasher safe, recycled glass crockery is a durable, long-lasting eco option for your table.

🍃 Bamboo – plates can be created from this grass in one of two ways: firstly, by being cut into small strips that are wound round a mould then glued together (with a non-toxic glue) to create a pattern of concentric circles. This is then covered with a protective clear lacquer on the inside and optionally decorated with vibrant colours on the exterior. Alternatively, the bamboo fibres are pulped and mixed with a biodegradable resin binder – 80% bamboo and

20% resin – to create a dark brown speckled material that is then moulded into cups, plates and bowls. When bamboo crockery reaches the end of its life, it can be composted rather than sent to landfill.

❋ Vintage plates – these are always an option for those on a budget, market lovers or the avid collector. It is always easy to pick up sets of vintage crockery and easier still to get hold of individual plates. If you are going for the latter option, my tip is to pick a colour, pattern or style and buy only that to create a cohesive collection – be it a particular shade, a floral pattern or even a style from a specifc era, such as the 1960s.

GLASSWARE

As glass bottles are so ubiquitous, the best eco choice of drinking glass is that made from reformed, crushed recycled glass. The styles and designs available are much improved from the early chunkier options, with the most current designs being slender and elegant. Again they have a slight greenish tinge to them.

Glasses are also produced directly from reused bottles – the top section is sliced off to create a tumbler from the remaining bottom half. Whilst these were innovative at the time of invention, they now seem rather crude and are, in a way, the first generation of eco products.

Being both durable and endlessly recyclable as a material, stainless steel spun into cups could always be an option. Although it has a relatively high embodied energy, its hardwearing quality means that it can be used for years and years. Created and used largely in Asia, stainless steel cups are available mostly as tumblers in ethnic

food shops. They may well complement an overall table setting, used as water goblets when mixed with other glassware.

You will also find that markets and secondhand shops are teeming with old glassware, just waiting for someone with a good eye to carefully put sets together. Again, these collections work best when you group together specific sets of glasses such as round wine glasses, small shot glasses or crystal goblets – their similarity and differences will play off each other wonderfully on your table.

CUTLERY

Cutlery may be best made from stainess steel – being so hardwearing and easy to use gives it a long lifespan. Again, as stainless steel is highly recyclable, it often has recycled content. You will also find that being such an adaptable material, stainless steel is available in a wide variety of designs to suit almost every taste. When you have finally finished with it, you can take it to a charity shop or metal recycling yard for reprocessing.

For a touch of old-world glamour there is an enormous selection of vintage cutlery available. As long as you are okay with the idea of others having used it before you (much the same as in any restaurant) this is a great and affordable option. Secondhand cutlery may be silver-plated, have bone handles or even be in retro 1960s designs. Again, pick your era or style and stick to that for a cohesive look.

STORAGE JARS

Whether for cereals, pasta, oils or herbs, there is a good variety of storage options open to you made from clear recycled glass. This allows the products that you use to be continually in sight and adds to the style of your kitchen, giving it a more wholesome feel. Made in all shapes and sizes, recycled glass storage jars are robust and easy to use, often having cork lids to keep the contents fresh.

In an effort to reduce the products that you use in the kitchen, rather than wrapping food in tin foil or clingfilm it is worth investing in a good selection of reusable polypropylene plastic boxes. These are wonderfully multi-functional – good for use in fridges, freezers and even picnics – and can be easily recycled once you have finished with them.

COOKING PANS AND UTENSILS

Over the years there have been a number of scares about the materials that we use to cook with and their effect on our health. Aluminium pans were thought to contribute to the onset of Alzheimer's disease, through the ingestion of the metal. However, there has been a vast amount of research carried out on this subject and current expert thinking is that there is no straightforward connection to be concerned of.

However, there is far more conclusive evidence of toxins associated with the use of non-stick pans. Their slippery coating contains substances such as PTFE and PFOA, which are known carcinogens and off-gas toxins when taken to high temperatures. This can happen if a pan boils dry or when frying foods but is more likely when the surface is worn and scratched.

Whilst these toxins are undetectable by humans, they can be ingested and collect in the body. They are also very dangerous to domesticated birds, who can die within a few minutes of direct contact to the fumes. So not only think twice about keeping your pet parrot in the kitchen, but consider using alternative cookware, such as stainless steel pans and ceramic baking dishes.

You may also wish to reevaluate your cooking utensils, which may be made from PVC-containing thalate plasticisers that make plastic flexible and bendy. Again these can be toxic when they degrade through heat and use. Instead use wooden utensils made from an FSC source that will not melt, poison you or scratch the bottom of your pans.

CHOPPING BOARDS

As well as having a wonderful wholesome feel, which is great when you are cooking, many types of timber have good anti-bacterial qualities so, from a practical point of view, wood makes for excellent chopping boards. With a wide selection for sale, it is worth checking that the wood is sourced from a well-managed sustainable source and is FSC certified. Alternatively look for newer selections of bamboo chopping boards, which will also have anti-bacterial qualities, and are likely to be affordable due the speed of the grasses' growth.

OPPOSITE Keep an open mind to alternative decorating ideas when designing your kitchen; do not be afraid to break with convention. This practical family home utilises easy-clean, professional freestanding kitchen units in conjunction with robust stainless steel trolleys on castors for storage. The industrial-style light fittings along with the sleek grey floor complete the warehouse feel of the space, which is softened by the warm wood dining table and pops of bright colour brought in by the homewares, not to mention the weekly shopping lists scrawled across the blackboard-painted feature wall.

BATHROOMS

BATHROOMS ARE OFTEN CRAMMED
INTO THE TINIEST SPACES WITHIN
THE HOME, YET AFTER THE
KITCHEN, IT IS WHERE WE USE THE
MOST RESOURCES – WATER, GAS
AND ELECTRICITY. SO DESPITE ITS
HUMBLE PROPORTIONS, THIS ROOM
HAS A POTENTIALLY EMBARRASSING
CARBON FOOTPRINT.

OPPOSITE For designers, the bathroom is an exciting yet complex space, where function and style must combine; but it is now also essential to exert an environmental consciousness when planning a bathroom. This bathroom feels luxurious but conceals its eco features. From flow-restricting taps to a generous-sized window that allows light to flood in, to a handheld shower mixer in the bath that helps to save water. The vintage wicker chair makes this a space to spend time in and relax.

A bathroom is a highly functional space, where all materials used must be durable. Although expensive to fit, cutting corners may ultimately cost you dear as bathroom fixtures and fittings have to endure daily dousings of water, soap and other cleaning agents. Considering the average bathroom suite is replaced every eight years, what happens to your old fittings is crucially important. If you can minimise the items that you must replace, all the better. Try giving your old bathroom a makeover – a fresh coat of paint, clean grout around the tiles, new taps, a replacement toilet seat, pristine white towels and the addition of a plant can make the world of difference. If you must tackle a full refurbishment, recycle whatever you can. In addition, remember that a vibrantly coloured bathroom suite is a personal choice, reducing its wider popularity, so opt for classic white to extend your bathroom's appeal and lifespan.

TECHNOLOGY, NATURE AND VINTAGE

Due to its highly practical nature the bathroom relies heavily on technological advances to minimise its use of resources. From a design angle, the bathroom is a private area and one of the more sensory spaces of the home so nature can also play a key role, offering up sensual materials to create a spa-like experience in even the most meagre of spaces. The materials play an important role in physically stimulating or soothing our bodies; it is where we both refresh ourselves in the mornings and relax after a long day at work. While the hardworking nature of a bathroom offers little opportunity for the introduction of vintage, an old leather armchair nestled into a corner or an ornate wall mirror will go a long way to soften the harder edges of the space and add character.

WATER-SAVING DEVICES

Until recently we have assumed our access to water is infinite – it is cheap, plentiful and, hey it does seem to rain a lot, so why should we care how much we use? Remember that we use 150 litres of water per person per day, and around 49 litres of that is in personal washing, (think basins, baths and showers) whilst we flush another 45 litres of fresh drinking-quality water down the toilet. These water usage statistics are both staggering and shocking.

Anticipated water shortages are set to be a global problem, but what can you do at home? Whether you are tackling a complete refit or want to reduce the impact of existing fittings, there are a number of water-saving devices to incorporate into your bathroom. We pay for cold water twice and hot water 3 times – once to buy it, once to heat it and finally to dispose of it – so water-saving devices make sense financially, with a short payback period. It is therefore well worth considering and implementing the following tips:

LOW-COST WAYS TO SAVE WATER
- Take short showers instead of daily baths.
- Turn off the tap while brushing your teeth.
- Fit flow restrictors to tap valves.
- Turn down taps' water supply valves.
- Fit a cistern displacement device to your toilet.
- Turn down your boiler's water temperature.
- Use a shower timer.

HIGHER-COST WAYS TO SAVE WATER
- Fit low-flow basin taps.
- Fit a low-flow showerhead.
- Fit an efficient syphon toilet cistern.
- Fit a grey water recycling system.

LOW-FLOW TAPS

Taps are potentially wasteful devices. Leaving a tap on while brushing your teeth squanders a minimum of six litres of water per minute, but may be as much as 20 litres. Furthermore, a dripping tap can waste a staggering 5,500 litres of water over a year, so doing simple repairs like replacing a washer makes significant reductions.

A simple water-saving tip is to turn down the isolating valve on each tap's supply pipe. Get the balance right and in a few days you will barely notice the reduction yet you will save water and money. If you have a combination boiler, take care not to turn down the valve to the hot tap so much that the boiler does not turn on. An alternative to reduce water flow is to fit an aerator, which simply screws on to the end of your existing tap. This restricts the flow, mixes the water with air to give the impression of the same flow rate. However, you will need aerators at different sizes for each tap, so it can get fiddly.

Whilst turning down the isolating valves simply restricts the actual flow of water (rather like putting your finger over the end of the tap), a flow restrictor will also regulate it, and can be used with either existing or new taps. Flow restrictors take the place of the isolating valve (located halfway up the water pipe under the basin). These flow regulating valves reduce the flow of the water and deliver a constant 6 litres of water per minute. If you are buying new taps, consider mono block mixing taps with an aerating spray flow, delivering 6 litres per minute. Alternatively, use a state-of-the-art two step tap delivering either an 80% water saving at the first setting or turn it to full flow – which encourages simple water saving every day.

RIGHT Creating a wet room is a sophisticated way to utilise bathroom space that would otherwise feel quite small. Use a flow restrictor or low-flow showerhead system for a luxurious drenching yet water-efficient shower.

SHOWERS

In general, taking a short shower is a more efficient way of refreshing yourself than a bath. On average a shower uses around 30 litres of water, just two-fifths of the 80 litres used by a bath. In reality, people who have a shower will use it more frequently than those who bath.

The real eco enemy is the power shower. In just five minutes it can use more water than a bath, plus it uses electricity to pump the water – two hits to the environment and your pocket in one. You do not necessarily have to compromise on luxurious showers to reduce your water usage as there are a couple of good options available.

Firstly, fit a flow restrictor to the water supply pipe, which keeps the flow rate at a steady 6 or 9 litres per minute. However, you must check that your showerhead will be appropriate for a reduced flow rate otherwise you may end up with large dribbles of water rather than a spray.

The second, and possibly better, option is to fit a purpose-designed low-flow aerating showerhead that will discharge around 75% less water than a conventional showerhead. I have one of these myself and love the luxurious soft drenching effect as the water is sent out in droplets rather than as a continuous stream.

TOILETS

The average toilet uses 9 litres of clean drinking water per flush, and accounts for 30% of our water use – 45 litres a day per person! The simplest way to reduce this is to fit a water displacement device to your toilet – a semi-rigid plastic bag that sits in the cistern and holds water otherwise flushed down the toilet – saving around 1 litre per flush.

Alternatively retrofit a dual flush conversion kit to your existing siphon cistern. Simple to fit and effective, they only release water into the pan for as long as the handle is held down. These can be bought online and can save up to 50% of water used. For a total refit, install a super-efficient toilet bowl and cistern. Experts recommend efficient dual flush 'siphon' cisterns (the type with a handle) which will use 4 and 2.7 litres respectively, rather than dual flush 'valve' systems (the type with a push button flush plate) which have been proven to leak and waste water.

BATHS

It is clear that a traditional bath still adds value to a property, even if it does conflict with the eco interior designer's best water-saving intentions. From a quality-of-life perspective, it is difficult to beat a luxurious soak in the bath after a long day. Plus if you have children, not having a bath tub can make life very difficult. So with this in mind, what is your best option?

Very simply, choosing a small bath – for example, a 170cm by 70cm model – over many of the oversized tubs available will instantly lead to a reduction in water usage each time the bath is filled. As baths are generally filled to a required level, there is little point in fitting low-flow taps or flow restrictors. Simply take less baths.

If you have only a limited amount of space, the obvious option is to plump for a combined bath and shower in junction with a screen. This could simply be a conventional tap with a shower hose attachment and a fabric screen hung from a rail. But if you plan to refit your bath, opt for an aerating low-flow shower with a folding glass screen. Be sure to choose a bath with a reasonable standing area and relatively vertical sides to reduce the chances of anyone slipping over.

When considering style, a double-ended tub with centrally placed taps allows two people to share a bath, encouraging a touch of water-wise romance. Otherwise, when making your choice remember that at the end of its useful life a cast-iron or steel bath can be taken to the scrap metal merchant to be recycled (you will even get a little money back for the former) but an acrylic bath is made from a petro-chemical plastic and will only end up in landfill.

Alternatively you could look to buy a vintage free-standing bath, which will add a luxurious touch of glamour to your bathroom. These can date from 1880 onwards with the claw-footed roll-top bath being a favourite for many. These can be bought from reclamation yards or even online, but be sure to check the enamel coating is undamaged and that the fitting holes are of a standard diameter. Be warned – some of these cast-iron baths can be extremely heavy so check their weights and the dimensions of your floor joists before purchase.

GREY WATER SYSTEMS

If we were to think carefully about our bathroom water usage – it would seem odd that we just allow bath, shower and basin water to flow away, when it is still perfectly usable for flushing the toilet. There are now a number of systems on the market that recirculate waste water to a storage tank (that holds around 100 litres), where it is skimmed and filtered before being used in the flushing of the cistern – theoretically reducing your water usage by 30%.

One of the main problems with grey water recycling is the presence of any chemicals, detergents and dirt in the water. Combined with the fact that it may well be warm, grey water is an ideal breeding ground for bacteria. Grey water either needs to be treated with chemicals (which can be environmentally harmful) or it can only be kept for few days after which time it will go stale. Also, as the water is contaminated it can only be used in relatively small quantities in the garden or on plants.

In theory, grey water recycling systems make sense. However, in reality it is probable that the costs associated with installing such a system domestically would outweigh the savings made from the reduction in water usage, making the payback period lengthy. A low-cost alternative is to fix a pipe with a tap to your bath waste, for use on the garden straight after washing.

OPPOSITE LEFT Choosing a small-sized basin is an easy way to reduce water usage. Simply put, a smaller basin means less water is needed every time the basin is filled.

OPPOSITE RIGHT Where space is at a premium, consider a smaller, space-saving toilet, which can be wall hung. Because the dual flush cistern is concealed and the bowl hovers above the floor, allowing you to see all the way back to the wall, an illusion of greater space is created.

WALLS

Due to the destructive qualities of water and condensation, walls in the bathroom must be scrupulously protected. A cheap quick fix is to coat all surfaces with thick gloss paint, but this will fill the space with high levels of VOCs (see page 65) that off-gas toxic residues and lead to breathing problems and allergic reactions. In addition, paint protects a surface for only a short time before it starts to peel and crack.

A much better solution is to part-tile and part-paint walls. The tiles allow any water to run off quickly, reducing damp levels. Some eco paints mark when splashed, so a good option is to use a natural eggshell paint that is mark resistant and hardwearing without the toxic chemicals.

FLOORS

Due to the bathroom's demanding conditions, flooring options are more limited than in other areas. Whilst bathroom flooring should feel good underfoot, it needs to be hardwearing, water resistant and able to deal with variations in moisture content. Additionally it needs to coordinate with the colour scheme of your bathroom; it is important visually, whether creating sleek lines or adding a textural finish.

🍃 Linoleum – one of the cheapest options, wide rolls mean that a bathroom could be fitted without the need for joins, making it extremely hardwearing and waterproof.

🍃 Cork tiles – water repellent, square cork tiles can be transformed by cutting them straight in half to create rectangular tiles.

🍃 Ceramic tiles – hardwearing and cost effective, although without such good environmental credentials. Cold to the touch, so use with a bathmat or underfloor heating.

🍃 Sold timber – susceptible to the changing moisture levels, leading it to swell and contract. Counteract this by fitting expansion cavities under skirting boards.

🍃 Rubber tiles – hardwearing yet soft, with a contemporary feel. Available in a selection of surface textures with good anti-slip properties.

🍃 Recycled rubber flooring – available in a roll to create a seamless floor.

LEFT Bathroom design has become an increasingly exciting area in recent years. New materials, such as ecoresin panels with encapsulated water reeds, as seen in the wall panels behind this shallow yet wide basin, have brought a myriad of sensual textures into what was once a conservative space; it is now possible to create an exotic spa feel within your own home.

OPPOSITE For rooms where space is not an issue, a freestanding bath makes a strong design statement. However, a generous bath need not be wasteful when it comes to water usage if a grey water system recycles spent bath water into toilet cisterns for flushing.

ABOVE This bathroom combines a small
contemporary water-saving basin set on a natural,
textural wooden plinth. The candelabra adds a touch
of vintage elegance and romance to this sensuous
bathing space.

LIGHTING

To create a truly multi-functional space that refreshes you in the morning and relaxes you after an exhausting day, maximise natural light levels and install three types of artificial lighting. All too often bathrooms have a cool atmosphere, due in part to the large amount of hard surfaces – tiled floors and walls – that creates an echoey environment but also to the wall colour and limited light available through what is usually a small window. As with any space, maximising the natural light (see pages 16 and 32) is the key to reducing the environmental impact of your bathroom's electricity usage. Now you may baulk at the idea of three lighting types but, believe me, the effects are worth it; good lighting design transforms a bathroom from an invigorating space to a calming spa. Good general lights, such as ceiling-mounted spotlights distributed evenly, are essential; task lighting above the basin mirror allows you to see yourself clearly; and lastly soft mood-enhancing lights create tranquil space.

GENERAL LIGHTING

Bathrooms are zoned into areas of safety; the nearer the water-bearing item, such as the shower, the higher the safety covering of the light must be to lower the risk of electrocution. As a result, the majority of bathrooms have recessed spotlights as opposed to ceiling-mounted pendant bulbs. Unless these lights have been recently upgraded the chances are that they will either be conventional tungsten bulbs or halogen spotlights, both of which have relatively high energy usages and short lives (see pages 84–9). In addition ceiling-mounted halogen spotlights create a harsh unflattering light, which increases the shadows under the eyes and the appearance of wrinkles – not good at all as you prepare to leave the house and want to feel your best. If you do have the former, tungsten bulbs can now be replaced by long-life, energy-saving fluorescent bulbs, available in a wide range of shapes and sizes – enough to replace all conventional bulb types.

If you have tired of the harsh light and low lifespan of conventional halogen spotlights, you have a couple of options. Firstly, they can be replaced with long-life, low-energy LEDs, although they have yet to make a direct size-for-size replacement for halogen bulbs, meaning they will stick out by 1cm from the old fittings. Alternatively replace the halogen fittings with LED spotlight fittings and warm white bulbs. You will need to budget for these, as the brighter bulbs can be pricey. However, they will use considerably less energy and will not need replacing as often. Specify the correct drivers (like conventional ballasts) and switching mechanisms and they can also be made into dimmable, mood-enhancing lights.

Fluorescent tubes have a reputation for harsh and unforgiving lighting, but if concealed they can give out a useful, even wash of softer reflected light – perfect for general lighting in the bathroom. Conceal them in wall recesses or above fitted cupboards so the actual bulb is not visible and ensure they cannot be touched.

TASK LIGHTING
Much like in the dressing rooms of actors, task lighting is best placed at eye level around the bathroom mirror, evenly lighting the face with no harsh shadows. A number of mirrors are

now available with built-in top or side lighting, activated by a conventional switch or drawstring pull. These are most likely to be compact fluorescent tubes but may also be single spotlights, which should ideally be low-energy LEDs. Refrain from being too creative with these lights – it is best to avoid vintage fittings – as they must be properly concealed in order to protect yourself from electrocution.

ADDITIONAL MOOD LIGHTING
However, if you want to take your lighting a stage further think about incorporating some fixed low-energy and low light-level fittings. Floor-level recessed wall lights (similar to stair lights) work wonderfully dotted around the perimeter of the bathroom to gently light a space, whilst making it safe to walk around. These will reflect softly off the floor and look great combined with a textural tile or timber floorcovering.

Alternatively if you have the space, consider a simple domestic LED fibre-optic system fitted into the ceiling above the bath. This twinkling light unit gives the effect of a starry sky at night, soothing away the stresses of the day. Mood lights work well when fitted to a ceiling-mounted infra-red sensor, which will detect your movement and switch on the light, as you enter the room at night – allowing the lights to operate without fumbling for the switch or temporarily blinding you as the main lights are switched on. They can simply be set to operate for short periods, meaning that lights are not left on in the middle of the night.

FURNITURE

If you have the space, additional furniture can transform your bathroom from a functional space to a luxurious one. The addition of a vintage chair will take the harder edges off the strong lines of a bathroom, and also provide space for you to add additional fabric items such as throws and cushions. They can also be useful to hold clothes and towels as you bath.

If you do not have space for a bigger chair, why not consider finding a low stool or even a small old folding chair, which will simply fold up when not in use? I love old folding military chairs, as they have a wonderful patina of age and wear in their structure and the canvas fabric materials.

TOWELS, BATHROBES AND MATS

After a good soak, wrapping yourself up in soft eco towels is a must. Investigate organic fairtrade cotton towels that will not contain chemical residues or have had a negative impact on the environment, or the communities that have grown the fabrics. Alternatively you can look at pure linen towels which will be absorbent but may be rather abrasive. Or lastly a great new alternative is towels made of bamboo fibre (woven onto an organic cotton backing sheet); they are wonderfully soft and fluffy, three times more absorbent than cotton and their natural anti-bacterial quality stops them from getting mouldy when damp. Due to bamboo's sustainable qualities and speed of growth, these are the towels of the future. Again bath robes and mats are available in a similar range of fabrics from organic cottons, to linen to bamboo.

CANDLES

The simplest mood lighting for a bathroom is the humble candle – its gentle, flickering glow creates a warm, calm atmosphere. Seize the opportunity to add a touch of vintage by styling your bathroom with an ornate candelabra or chandelier (which could simply hang from the ceiling on a hook). In this unconventional setting, with its decorative detailing contrasted with the clean lines of the bathroom, it could look stunning – making a simple candlelit bath a romantic moment.

But be sure that you use natural soy or palm oil candles that use essential oils if they have fragrances and no artificial scents. These will not contain petrochemical products, which will release a black sooty smoke known to contain toxins and carcinogens (see page 89).

NATURAL SOAPS AND BATH OILS

There is now a wide variety of companies specialising in natural soaps and oils. On the whole, these will be better for sensitive skin, and are made with essential oils, and natural organic ingredients. By contrast, conventional bathing products can contain artificial scents, animal products and petrochemicals, and can contain toxic parabens – not very relaxing when you start to think about it! Remember it's not just about the products that you will be using on your skin but also about how they were made and what goes down the plug hole into the environment afterwards.

MIRRORS

No bathroom is finished without the aid of a good mirror – essential for perfect grooming and making sure that you look your best before you leave in the morning. In a space that can all too often be dominated by technology and strong lines, it is worth considering a mirror that will restore some character to the space. Vintage or decorative mirrors can do this simply for you and will add extra richness to even the most humble of bathrooms. It is easy to track down old mirrors, but if you feel that they have too much detail or you do not like the ornate finish it can work well to paint the frame in the wall colour of your bathroom, which will help to tone down the overall effect, adding a subtle opulence. If you prefer to buy a new mirror and want to choose one with a wooden frame, check that is made from FSC-sourced timber.

ABOVE This bathroom has a wonderfully wholesome feel. It balances technology (in modern taps fitted with flow restrictors), nature (in the timber materials) and vintage (in the accessories). Now if only that lightbulb were changed to a low-energy version, it would be perfect!

BEDROOMS

WE SPEND MORE TIME IN THE BEDROOM THAN ANYWHERE ELSE (PROVIDING YOU LIKE A GOOD NIGHT'S SLEEP... IN YOUR OWN BED). A BEDROOM IS A SANCTUARY WHERE WE SLEEP, RELAX AND READ. BEYOND THESE DREAMY PASTIMES, A BEDROOM SERVES A VARIETY OF PRACTICAL FUNCTIONS, INCLUDING STORAGE AND DRESSING. IT IS A SPACE TO RELAX IN AND A PLACE TO PREPARE FOR THE DAY AHEAD.

From an environmental perspective, the bedroom does not demand as obviously high a level of resources as either the kitchen or the bathroom. However, it is still a space that needs careful ecological thought when considering its decoration and furnishings. Of course, style plays an all-important role when planning a bedroom.

ABOVE A modern take on the four-poster bed in cool, machined steel, with fairtrade cotton bed linen and an assortment of vintage furniture and antique objects all add up to the quintessential eco-chic bedroom.

The main steps that you need to take for an eco-conscious bedroom are to:

● Cut down on energy use, in the form of heating and lighting.

● Minimise toxins in materials and finishes.

● Reduce the levels of dust, which can lead to asthma and allergies.

🍂 Use fairtrade (and organic) fabrics for all bed linens, thereby easing your eco conscience for a really good night's sleep.

A bedroom being a space that requires few technological resources, its style relies more heavily on the use of the natural and the vintage. That said, as with any room in the house, making it environmentally efficient will also make it a more comfortable place to spend time in. So you will want to:

● Reduce any draughts that may result from badly fitting windows. If your windows are leaking cold air, fit draught-excluding brushes or foam strips. As a temporary measure – because it may prevent you from opening the window – fit secondary double glazing, such as an acrylic plastic sheet or even polythene film that is tensioned across the face of the window with a hairdryer.

● Reduce heat loss from chimneys and fireplaces either by boarding up the flue or buying an inflatable plastic layered balloon. When inflated, the balloon will fill the lower section of the flue, blocking draughts and stopping any soot from dropping down the chimney into the fireplace.

● Retain a low level of ventilation within the room to prevent moisture and condensation building up in the room and creating mould.

● Create the right lighting levels using low-energy lightbulbs, preferably LEDs.

● Fit thermostatic valves to your bedroom radiators, regulating the temperature to an ideal 18°C. Such valves can be retrofitted to replace any existing on/off radiator valves.

● Fit reflective panels behind each radiator to kick the heat forward and prevent it from simply rising upwards – these are available from most DIY and hardware stores.

🍂 Insulate windows with thick curtains, which will also help to prevent heat radiating into the room during the summer.

A greater grounding quality can be harnessed by using natural materials in the bedroom – textural elements that help create a healthy space free of chemicals and toxins. A variety of natural materials can be used for bedroom furniture, floorings, wall surfaces and fabrics.

The use of vintage items in the bedroom imparts an individual identity onto the space – after all, it is your private area, so make it unique to you, with treasured items that you enjoy and that say something about who you are. Personal collections and objects displayed in your bedroom will reflect you and your experiences, allowing you to relax into a space that suits you perfectly. Vintage items can also add a romantic quality, allowing you to revel in a sense of nostalgia about your life or shared experiences with your partner, be they mementoes of time spent together or pieces chosen in antique stores, markets or on travels. Even in a bedroom, the softening effect of vintage pieces on the harder edges of a clean-cut contemporary space is useful. A worn leather armchair might be juxtaposed with a modern storage unit, for example, to set up an enticing visual contrast.

BEDS

As the most prominent piece of furniture in the room, your bed is the focal point. Beds are also the most well-used pieces of furniture in your entire home, so it is essential that you make the right choice. From an environmental point of view, you need to consider both aspects of your bed; the mattress as well as the frame itself.

Both the nature and vintage options offer sound environmental choices for beds. Natural timber frames supply a robust texture and warmth; however, they must carry FSC certification (see page 57). If not, they could have been made with illegally logged timber from an unsustainable source, such as virgin forests. Just how well would you sleep, knowing that your bed may have had a harmful and unnecessary impact on the environment?

Vintage bed frames have been popular for a number of years, as they lend an air of nostalgic romance, though they need not be overtly feminine. Search in antique shops and at auction houses or online auction sites, but do be aware that a metric-sized mattress may not exactly fit an imperial-sized bed, so check carefully.

Some typical vintage beds you may find are:
❀ Ornate wrought-iron beds – curvaceous metalwork adds a fairytale Princess feel.
❀ Classic panelled timber beds – solid, plain and simple.
❀ Decorative upholstered French-style beds – opulent and elegant, strong and yet romantic.
❀ Intricately carved wooden Art Deco style beds – for a real vintage look.
❀ Simple cast-iron bedsteads with vertical rails – they can be elegant, but also suit a

shabby chic look. These are best stripped or sand-blasted, to remove any possible traces of old lead paintwork, before being repainted.

Alternatively, construct your own bed frame: take pleasure in making something that you will use every day. That is not to say it must be expertly crafted, but if thoughtfully designed a bed can speak volumes about the character of your most personal space. Previously I have constructed beds from wooden shipping pallets, a reclaimed shop display system (much like a small scaffold system) and timber salvaged from film sets. Searching out the material adds to the excitement of creating something unique.

Currently my bed is made from a futon base with sides clad in reclaimed timber floorboards to give it a soft, aged feel. The whole frame has concealed legs set back from the sides to convey the impression the bed is floating, rather like a magical flying carpet. To enhance this effect, the bed is underlit with a string of low-energy fairy lights that twinkle at night and amplify the sensation that the bed is hovering, ready to whisk me off to the mystical Land of Sleep.

When making your own bed frame, ensure the mattress will be properly supported by building in wooden slats with gaps of less than 5cm between them. These slats can be attached to an existing frame or form the basis of a new frame. Keep an open mind when considering the bed's headboard and legs; both elements offer a chance to be creative. Being a predominantly horizontal plane, any vertical elements of your bed frame may really stand out. Consider the following sources when searching for materials for your bed frame:

❋ RECLAIMED TIMBER YARDS – for old doors, aged floorboards, disused pallets, gnarled pieces of wood or turned newel posts from stairs. Take care not to use any materials that may have previously been coated in toxic preservatives, such as creosote.

❋ CAR SCRAP YARDS – for enormous shock-absorbing springs and many other bits and pieces, perhaps even a retro car dashboard.

❋ SCRAP METAL YARDS – for all sorts of inspirational items, such as metal panels, scaffold parts, old signage and trolleys with oversized wheels.

❋ MARKETS – for antique bed frames that can be incorporated into new designs, vintage screens, reclaimed furniture that can be re-appropriated, vintage fabrics for coverings and an amazing assortment of other pieces.

MATTRESSES

Considering the amount of time we spend lying on our mattresses, it is essential to choose one made with both health and comfort in mind. Conventional mattresses are not only treated with fire retardants and so contain residues of chemicals, but other toxins are used in the growing and manufacturing of its fabrics, including insecticides and pesticides. An organic mattress or futon will benefit not just you, but also the environment within which the materials were produced in the first place.

Constructed in a similar way to a conventional mattress, an organic mattress simply uses natural materials, such as wool and cotton, which are sourced from a carefully monitored chain of suppliers none of which will have used the commonplace cocktail of chemicals in their production. What is more, they also reduce the need for harmful fire retardants by using non-combustible materials, such as wool.

Although more expensive, the alternative to an organic mattress is a natural latex mattress. Tapped from rubber trees, latex has a unique elasticity and flexibility allowing your body to be evenly supported. Considered hypoallergenic, these mattresses are free from animal hair, chemical additives and are resistant to dust mites, so are recommended for allergy sufferers or those with skin conditions. The latex is generally encased in an organic cotton removable sleeve that can be washed, thereby further reducing the amount of dust build-up.

Because it is warmer to sleep on than a conventional mattress, you will need only a thin duvet with a latex mattress so you can turn down

the heating in your bedroom; they are the perfect eco solution being better for you and reducing the energy needed to heat your home at night.

If you are not planning to change your mattress but are concerned about rising levels of allergies then you may want to consider getting your mattress cleaned regularly. Over the course of the year your body will shed around one kilogram of skin and 260 litres of perspiration. Combined with the warm conditions in your bed, this makes it the ideal breeding ground for dust

ABOVE Use vintage to create an atmosphere that suits your home. In this case, the owners have given their bedroom a simple, yet romantic French feel.

mites: it is estimated that the average double mattress contains over one million mites. So whilst I know you do not really want to think about this, it is the dust mite droppings that are directly responsible for respiratory problems, such as asthma, and skin allergies, such as eczema. Every time you move around in your bed these particles are likely to be inhaled.

If you are concerned – and really you should be – look to reduce the amount of dust mite droppings within your bed by vacuuming it thoroughly once a week. Alternatively try to reduce the moisture content of your bed, which encourages the mites, by airing it on a daily basis – this is also a good excuse not to make your bed each morning.

Alternatively there are a number of naturally based sprays that can be used directly onto the mattress to kill off the mites, after which they can be vacuumed up. This process will have to be regularly repeated so as to prevent continued build-up.

STORAGE

Good storage should be the first thing you think of when planning your ideal bedroom – work out what you need to store, consider whether you have adequate space to house it all and ensure the storage is located in the right part of the room. For a clutter-free bedroom you will need to devote at least 10% of your floor area to storage. This may take on different forms – from built-in cupboards, to freestanding units, dressing tables, bedside tables, shelves and even under-bed storage boxes. Being so prolific and visible in the bedroom, all these forms of storage ought to be carefully thought about.

BUILT-IN CUPBOARDS

An efficient use of space, built-in cupboards maximise the available storage to create high-level, easy-access and low-level options for clothes, shoes and other items. Cupboards enclose your clothes, cutting down on surfaces that can collect dust, so reducing dust mites.

With large areas of flat board needed to construct such furniture, MDF (medium density fibreboard) is commonly used as it is readily available, easy to handle and finishes well. However, MDF has a high formaldehyde resin content – about 10% of its weight – which is harmful when breathed in. When MDF is cut, it sheds particles and over time it can off-gas formaldehyde toxins, known carcinogens. Ensure that you or your carpenter specify ZF-MDF (zero formaldehyde medium density fibreboard) when ordering materials. Although more expensive, this is a much safer option. In addition you will want to finish the ZF-MDF in natural paint that contains no VOCs, such as a water-based eggshell.

As ZF-MDF is entirely flat fronted and smooth, you may want to add decorative detail in the form of the handles, which you could collect as vintage pieces from markets or antique shops. Even if they are not all matching, the variety will add quirky character to the overall effect.

FREESTANDING FURNITURE

Simpler to install than built-in storage, freestanding cupboards can be a useful storage option. Although they are less costly, they are also less efficient with the available space. We have all become accustomed to buying flatpack storage units, and spending dreaded weekends constructing them. Once assembled and in situ they provide a storage quick fix but have you considered the materials used to make them? Their low quality and strength means that the average lifespan for these pieces is short. Once you have decided you no longer want them, they have a low second-hand desirability so the only choice is to send them to landfill. And then there is the discarded packaging to consider. It is all a frustrating waste to me.

If you do plan to buy a new storage cupboard, then make sure it has the FSC logo applied to it. An exciting alternative is to spend a little time and energy searching for old but highly reusable storage cupboards in markets, online auction sites, second-hand or antique shops. What you will find is that there is an enormous variety, so you can pick from a selection of antique and later twentieth-century pieces that will offer a number of creative directions – now that is much more exciting.

OPPOSITE Re-appropriating old display cabinets from shops or haberdashers is a great way to show off any collection that you are proud of, and if that is clothing then it makes finding an item even easier.

ABOVE Flat-faced cabinets and wardrobes can easily be reinvigorated by covering the surfaces with wallpaper – to stunning effect.

OPPOSITE Make space for the things that are important to you; a bedroom is a very personal space and so it should reflect your passions, character and even life history.

ADDITIONAL STORAGE

Once the bulk of your clothes, shoes and toiletries are stored and out of sight, have some fun creating more unusual forms of storage for all those other bits and pieces, such as books, jewellery and photographs, that you will need to house in your bedroom. Keep your eyes open for anything that can be fixed to a wall or that will sit stably on the floor or tabletop. Of course you can buy sets of floating shelves or display cabinets but this is a chance to get creative:

❀ Aged timber or floorboards used as shelves.
❀ Wooden fruit boxes stacked or fixed to walls.
❀ Wooden wine cases or metal biscuit boxes.
❀ Vintage leather suitcases.
❀ Ornate metal brackets to use with shelves.
❀ Old wooden drawers piled up and fixed to one another – different sizes work well together.
❀ Old metal mesh cages – like old school shoe lockers.

To give an old cupboard or bedside table a new lease of life:

❧ Simply sand the piece down and then repaint it using natural VOC-free paints.
❀ If the piece is covered in layers of paint, sand it down removing uneven amounts of paint to give it a distressed look.
❀ Paint the interior a vibrant shocking colour for a real burst of energy.
❧ Paint a section in natural paints and cover another flat section with a matching wallpaper (perfect if you have left-over sections of wallpaper from a feature wall – it will coordinate the room).
❀ Give it a soft reflective touch by recovering the front in gold or silver leaf squares.
❧ Stencil an oversized motif of feathers, leaves or historic patterns onto the piece using natural paints – giving the effect of a piece of interior graffiti.
❀ Use upholsterers pins (smooth dome-headed nails) to create a series of dotted patterns – stylised flower or leaf motifs work well as the light catches them.
❀ Replace the door handles and legs with something more contemporary or eclectic such as vintage glass handles, or reclaimed cast-iron dragons feet from a roll-top bath.
❀ Use decoupage sections of cut-out paper, (such as magazine pages) to cover the exterior with, and then varnish to seal it.
❀ Make it glow – under-light the piece with fairy lights or a low-energy fluorescent strip light – it is fun to experiment.
❀ Use blackboard paint to create a surface you can write onto (best done where you have a solid floor surface below).

FABRICS

Fabrics play an essential role in softening a bedroom, helping to make the space more enticing. Not only are fabrics sensual and soft to the touch but they also absorb noise, reducing echoes and making a more relaxed acoustic environment. From a visual point of view, they add another layer to the design of your bedroom, providing accent colours, visual texture and importantly a chance to create an easy-to-change seasonal look without any great effort, expense or wastefulness. So for a long-lasting bedroom style, focus on neutral background colours for walls and floors and look to change the fabric accessories on a more regular basis.

WINDOW TREATMENTS

If you want to minimise the amount of fabrics to cut dust levels (and with it dust mites), veer towards simple roller blinds. These can be silver-backed or blackout blinds that reduce daylight and prevent heat entering the room when drawn. Alternatively consider wooden Venetian blinds or folding shutters (made from FSC certified timber, of course) that allow you to control the daylight levels within the space.

There is now an increasing market and availability in organic and fairtrade fabrics such as cotton, linen and hemp, which can be used as conventional fabrics. The difference being that these fabrics will not have been grown using insecticides, pesticides or will have contributed to unfair working practices – giving them a reduced environmental and social impact from the very outset (see pages 76–83). The benefit for you, apart from a reduced level of guilt, is that they also will not contain chemical residues that can put toxins into your bedroom.

An exciting alternative is to use vintage fabrics. For those who hate to sew or baulk at the expense of handmade or even ready-made options, this is the perfect way to bring a little urban eco chic into your home. Scour markets and second-hand shops or online auction sites for ready-made vintage curtains.

If chosen carefully these will be well-made pieces that are lined (adding extra insulation to your windows) and have curtain-fixing tape sewn on. Make sure that you have a tape measure and know the length and size of the window that you plan to cover – rolls of fabric seem deceptively long, but curtains that are too short will just look wrong. Overly long curtains however can add a sense of decadence as they drape luxuriously across the floor, but if you want a neater sense of precision then having curtains hemmed to size (or even sewing them yourself) is a relatively cheap and easy job to do. Consider too whether you will want to extend your curtain tracks past the window frames as, unless fully drawn back, thick curtains can reduce natural light levels.

Choosing the right vintage fabric type will have an impact on the style of your bedroom, so you will want to think carefully about where you are going with this. Choose from a selection of the following fabrics that are likely to be available:

OPPOSITE The simplicity of this space shows off the variety of vintage fabrics to wonderful effect, whilst the antique bed adds a real sense of grandeur, making the overall feel luxurious rather than nostalgic.

❀ Country florals and traditional chintzes – for old-fashioned feminine delicacy.

❀ Patchwork fabrics – for rustic 'granny chic'.

❀ Rich silky damasks – for opulent grandeur.

❀ Delicate lacework – for soft, filtered light and romantic feeling.

❀ Oriental silk – for mysterious exoticism.

❀ Vintage 1950s – for refined sophistication.

❀ Retro 1960s or 70s – for naïve playfulness.

❀ Plain velvets – for bold banks of colour.

❀ Old wool blankets (picnic style or army grey) – for utilitarian comfort.

BED LINENS

As bed linens are the fabrics closest to your skin while you sleep, it makes good sense to ensure your bed linen is as natural as possible, rather than full of toxins, and is produced in an ethical way. (See pages 76–83 for information on organic fairtrade cotton and bamboo.) Organic cotton fibres are also longer and softer than ordinary cotton fibres, which should give you an even better night's sleep, though personally, I sleep better just knowing the bed linen I use has been produced in a fairtrade manner – last thing at night it is easier to doze off with a clear conscience.

OPPOSITE Don't be afraid to dye vintage fabrics – sometimes it is simply the colour that is offputting. Better to give an item a new lease of life than to let it languish unused, plus the results are surprisingly satisfying.

BELOW Layer up plain white sheets with textural knits to add impact and warmth.

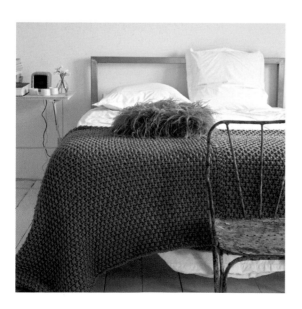

BEDSPREADS AND THROWS

Dressing a bed adds visual impact to the room, making the bed look and feel sumptuous. Buying a bedspread or throw can be surprisingly costly, particularly if you insist upon pure organic materials, however you will feel the benefit. Natural fabrics, such as organic wool, cashmere and alpaca, give a bed a warm cosy feel that you just will not want to leave. A more cost-effective method of adding impact is to use a recycled wool blanket (possibly even made from recycled jumpers), due to small quantities of the fabrics available these are produced in checked or tartan fabrics.

Alternatively look to use vintage fabrics to dress your bed. Whilst covering it in swathes of fabric may be overkill, think about a gentle layering process by adding fabrics just to the foot of the bed. You may be lucky enough to find patchwork fabric throws or why not consider making one up if your sewing skills are up to it. If the rest of the room is kept relatively free from decoration, strong colour and pattern, adding detailed vintage prints to a bed will work wonderfully. Updating vintage fabrics may just be a case of spending the time to dye them, for them to tie in with the rest of your bedroom's colour scheme. This can be carried out by hand or in the washing machine, but it is a good idea to check first of all that the fabric is natural (such as cotton or silk) and will take the dye.

Remember that using vintage pieces will add character and depth to this most personal of places – allowing you to suggest romance, history, and sophistication to your bedroom.

MIRRORS AND PICTURE FRAMES

Walls can be decorated with more than just natural paints so consider adding to them with mirrors and picture frames. Mirrors will provide you with an opportunity to make yourself look your best before you step out of the house, but of course also help to bounce light around your bedroom. Vintage mirrors will add depth and interest, their uneven reflective backing adding real depth and character to its appearance.

Being a private space, use your bedroom walls to display pictures of those you cherish. Whilst new frames are widely available, using an assortment of old frames will add individuality to every picture. To make the frames feel more contemporary, think about unifying them by painting each frame the same colour, this will highlight detail but make the differences subtler.

BEDROOM CHAIRS

If you have the luxury of space, adding a chair to your bedroom emphasises the fact that this is a pleasurable space for spending leisure time in rather than solely a place for sleeping in at night. Adding a place to sit gives the room a further dimension – somewhere contemplation and perhaps conversation can happen.

Having said that, we do not all have the luxury of enough space for a languorous chaise longue, so instead look for a small armchair or even a simple dining chair with arms. These can be dressed with cushions and throws to be made more inviting. If you are as messy as I am, bedroom chairs inevitably become clothes horses at night – cutting out the need to fold and hang clothes back in the cupboard – a lazy person's temporary wardrobe.

OPPOSITE Mirrors not only reflect views, they also help to bounce light back into spaces. In this case, the vintage bevelled edged mirrors add a romantic essence to this bedroom.

RIGHT Positioned in a bedroom, a single chair can be 'framed' by the space so invest in a chair that is a pleasure to look at – when it is not covered in clothes, that is.

CHILDREN'S ROOMS

FOR ANY PARENT, IT IS OF THE UTMOST IMPORTANCE THAT THEIR CHILD'S ROOM BE A SAFE SPACE FREE FROM TOXINS. BEYOND THAT, IT SHOULD BE A SPACE THAT IS FUN, INSPIRING AND ORGANISED. AND, OF COURSE, IT SHOULD HAVE A MINIMUM IMPACT ON THE ENVIRONMENT THAT THEY WILL ONE DAY INHERIT.

OPPOSITE As this child's room proves, it is possible to create a vibrant and stimulating space using natural VOC-free paints, eco-wallpapers and a range of vintage or recycled fabrics. The patchwork wall panels and fabrics give a creative and relaxed feel to this child's bedroom. Advantageously, any panel may be easily replaced if ever marked or damaged.

FLOORS

To your child, the floor is a surface to crawl over, play on and most likely (given a child's ignorance of germs) even eat off. Because a child has so much contact with the floor, it is important to cut out dust and toxins, especially as a child's immune system is not fully developed.

● Carpets are soft and cushioning, but they trap dust and are breeding grounds for mites, increasing the risk of allergies and asthma. Do away with carpets to reduce dust levels.

● Artificial-fibre carpets contain high levels of toxins, such as stain inhibitors, fire retardants and traces of pesticides. They will off-gas over time, especially when new.

● As an alternative to carpet, consider a rug (with an anti-slip mat) that can be readily cleaned and beaten outside to remove trapped dust. Buy one with a natural latex or hessian backing as artificial latex contains toxins. Plus, if it gets damaged, it will cost less to replace.

● Alternatively opt for 100% natural pure wool carpet. Wool is the easiest of the natural-fibre carpets to clean and will not contain toxins in its upper or lower layers. Have it treated with a natural toxin-free stain inhibitor. Regular and thorough vacuum cleaning will also help to keep dust levels down.

● Solid floors reduce dust levels, because they are easier to clean. But stay away from floors that contain artificial materials, such as MDF found in laminate floors, or layered floors, such as engineered floors. Instead, opt for a solid-material floor, such as solid timber, cork (which has a natural spring to it), natural rubber or linoleum.

● Avoid floorings stuck down with glues that off-gas formaldehyde as they dry. Specify natural non-toxic adhesives, such as natural latex.

FURNITURE

It is critical that you buy solid furniture. Not only is it likely to be harder wearing, but it will not contain toxins. Cheaper furniture is likely to be made from particleboard with a covering laminate of wood veneer, which uses a toxic formaldehyde glue to bond the wood particles together. Over time, this formaldehyde will off-gas into your child's sleeping area. Toxin-free solid wood should ideally be oiled, rather than finished with any VOC-containing varnishes or paints. If the retailer does not know whether an item is toxin free, simply do not take the risk.

BEDS

Your child's bed could be made from a steel frame or solid timber; both will be hardwearing and can eventually be recycled or sold on. Beware cheaper 'wooden' beds that are likely to be made of laminates and so can off-gas toxins directly onto your child's pillow.

MATTRESSES AND BED LINEN

Mattresses are a source of toxic materials and in a very short time harbour dust mites. So choose organic fibre materials to ensure that no toxins (such as fertilisers, herbicides fungicides and pesticides) come into contact with your child's bed. You can now find mattresses that are available which are made of natural organic materials, such as sheep's wool, natural latex and coir, to ensure that the application of toxic fireproofing substances are unnecessary.

As your child gets older, consider a latex mattress with washable covers to inhibit dust mites. These latex mattresses are expensive, however; so if you do opt for a conventional mattress, vacuum it thoroughly every week to keep dust mite levels down. Likewise, bed linen should come from an organic source. It is possible to buy fabrics, such as organic cotton and bamboo-fibre fabrics, that do not contain toxic chemical residues from their growth and processing (see pages 80–2).

TOYS

Throw out any PVC toys. PVC is damaging in its fabrication, involving dangerous cocktails of chemicals. To make PVC bendy, chemicals known as plasticisers are added, which have been shown to ill affect the liver, kidney, lungs and blood pressure, as well as the reproductive tract of boys. As PVC toys are often chewed, these toxins can be ingested. Instead buy wooden toys that are safe and will biodegrade.

OPPOSITE This child's bedroom does not have a single strong theme but rather pulls together lots of different fun natural and vintage elements.

RIGHT Vintage furniture will either have originally used a less toxic paint than modern equivalents or it will have had a chance to off-gas completely. This bureau offers space to work as well as the chance to display a collection of much-loved possessions.

LIVING ROOMS

THE LIVING ROOM IS THE KEY
SOCIAL SPACE IN YOUR HOME. IT IS
ALSO A PERSONAL ROOM, WHICH
CAN SPEAK VOLUMES ABOUT WHO
YOU ARE, THE INTERESTS YOU
HOLD, AND HOW YOU LIKE TO LIVE.
WHAT IS MORE, IT IS A MULTI-
FUNCTIONAL SPACE FOR RELAXING,
READING, WATCHING TELEVISION,
PLAYING AND ENTERTAINING.

Living spaces often contain high levels of
technology, so it is important to reduce the
room's electrical loading as much as possible.
It is also crucial to recognise that all this
technology has a distinct visual impact on the
room. With cables, plugs and an array of shiny
fascias, modern technology can lead to a high
level of clutter, which detracts from the focus of
the space. Our homes should embrace
technology, so that it is at the tips of our fingers
when we do need it, but does not impact on our
lives when we do not. We need to find ways of
cleverly integrating – and perhaps even
concealing – technology wherever possible.

Creating the perfect urban eco chic living room
relies on balancing our use of technology,
nature and vintage, to make a space that is at
once efficient, comfortable and characterful –
but the ultimate goal is to create a space that is
a pleasure to be in without impacting
unnecessarily on the environment.

ABOVE The living room of designer Lisa Whatmough is
peppered with her highly creative designs. She sources
neglected antiques, from armchairs to floor lamps, and

re-covers them in vintage fabrics. You may wonder how
she gets so many different colours and patterns to work
together; but somehow her artist's eye makes it happen.

ABOVE A wood-burning stove is a far more efficient way of heating a space than an open fire. Furthermore, this stove creates a visual focal point to the living room giving it a rustic sense of warmth – and prevents ash and soot from spreading over the room.

FIREPLACES AND STOVES

A fireplace creates a focal point within a living room, around which you can position sofas, chairs, tables and rugs. The flickering of real flames yields a restful quality. However, if you are intent on having an open fire, remember that up to 80% of the heat produced from conventional wood fires simply escapes up the chimney, so you cannot rely on it as part of a total heating system for your home.

A chimney acts as a funnel, designed to suck smoke up and out of your home. However, along with that smoke goes the majority of the heat produced by an open fire or, if the chimney is unused, by your central heating system. Unused fireplaces can be capped to stop air movement – although this is by no means a simple task as it involves accessing the uppermost part of your roof. Even so, you will still be heating the air inside the chimney breast. A better option is to seal the underside of the flue with a water-resistant plywood cover that prevents heat loss and dust falling down the chimney. Alternatively, fit a chimney balloon inflated inside the lower part of the chimney, which prevents heat loss whilst retaining a low level of ventilation to the room.

A gas-fired, coal-effect fire has a similar level of heat loss but with the added environmental downside of burning a carbon-heavy, non-renewable fuel. Consider instead a cast-iron or steel log-burning stove, which loses only around 20% of its heat up the chimney. For every four logs burnt on an open fire, just one is needed in a wood-burning stove to create the same heat output. This means fewer logs to chop and less ash to clean. In addition, wood is a carbon-neutral fuel – it releases the same carbon when burnt as it captures whilst it grows – so for conventional central heating it is far less damaging to burn than gas. Added to the fact that wood is cheaper than gas in relation to the energy it creates, wood-burning stoves are an excellent option when considering your whole heating plan. On the downside, wood-burning stoves can be more costly, so look online for second-hand models or simply regard it as a sound home investment.

There is an enormous variety of stoves on the market, many with glass fronts so you can still enjoy the visual glow of a real fire but with the added advantages. It is essential to remember that with all wood-burning stoves, you will need a constant source of ventilation and a properly installed flue system.

If you have neither a fireplace nor a hearth, an alternative may be a flueless fire. These use natural bio-fuel gel pots made of ethanol and propenol dervied from rape seed. Placed in a slide-out drawer under a series of coals or pebbles, when lit these bio-fuel gel pots create real flickering flames. The advantages are that you do not need a flue, which can let in draughts, 100% of the heat produced by the burners enters the room and no ash is produced – giving you the focal effect of flickering flames without the downsides of a conventional fire. As oxygen is still being burnt it is important to properly ventilate the room. These units can be simply hung on a wall or worked into a conventional-looking fireplace, creating a focal point for the room, diverting it away from the television. Each gel pot burns for around three hours, after which you simply refill the tins from a bottle.

WINDOW TREATMENTS

With living rooms often being sited on the ground floor, privacy may be an issue so there is a balance to be struck between obscuring windows and maximising the amount of natural light allowed to flood in. Whilst the normal rules to maximising natural light apply (see pages 16 and 32) here are some stylish ideas for screening windows whilst allowing light in:

● Sheer fabric roller blinds that pull upwards, leaving the upper sections free to let light in.
● Adjustable FSC timber Venetian blinds in a light colour or painted white.
● Fold-back shutters with louvres.
● Voile or sheer linen or muslin curtains.
● Opaque glass in lower window sections.
● Opaque window film adhered to the panes.
● Opaque screens made from any number of materials such as garden centre willow reed screens or even panels of thick tracing paper, weighted along the bottom edge.

LIGHTING

More often than not, general living room lights are centrally mounted pendants, which must be fitted with low-energy bulbs. These bulbs are now dimmable, making their light variable and mood enhancing. Alternatively, make a grand lighting statement with a vintage chandelier; simply refit it with low-energy candle bulbs to marry the old and new. General lights could also take the form of a spread of LED downlighters across the ceiling. Although intended as spotlights, LEDs will create a uniform spread of light when evenly spaced. Specify warm white LEDs, as standard LEDs are relatively blue, creating a colder feeling that is inappropriate for living spaces.

Sidelights and table lamps create an intimate atmosphere. They can transform a space from a brightly lit functional room into one of relaxed calm. Soft pools of light cast onto a side table or over the arm of a sofa entice you to sit and unwind. Low-level light alters the feel of the space, adding character, and being of a lower power they can also help to reduce your overall electrical usage. Consider ways of introducing mood-enhancing lighting into your living room:

● Low-energy LED spotlights directed onto pictures or architectural features.
● Ceiling-mounted coloured LED downlighters positioned to wash light down walls in soft scallop shapes.
● Strings of fairy lights wrapped around mirrors, picture frames, piled in frosted vases or around logs in the fireplace
● LED colour-changing table lights producing soft pulsing glows of differing shades
● Rope lights coiled beneath pieces of furniture such as chairs or sideboards.

OPPOSITE A variety of lights provide different levels of illumination to transform this room from a functional area (albeit lit by an opulent chandelier) into an intimate space cast in pools of light. Vintage light fittings are a great way to hide energy-saving bulbs and retain character.

FURNITURE

Furniture not only plays an important role in the style and comfort of your living room, it is also likely to be a significant financial outlay – with the primary investment being in your own relaxation. Eco-friendly furniture, particularly sofas and armchairs, has been strangely slow in coming onto the market. As this area of retail is so competitively priced, many retailers do not dare bring out a sofa that is substantially more expensive, even if it does carry an environmental label.

Another barrier to furniture with a low environmental impact is that regulations state upholstery must use fire retardants, many of which contain toxins. Whilst not every manufacturer uses all the following chemicals, some do. Be persistent in asking what any sofa contains and be aware of the chemicals that may poison your body as you sit. Be aware that an inexpensive sofa is likely to contain:

● Brominated fire retardants – applied to upholstery fabrics and curtains, these hormone disruptors get stored long term in the body.
● Phthalates – found in PVC, these can be absorbed by the body and cause liver damage, reproductive and respiratory problems.
● Formaldehyde – found in plywood, carpets and upholstery fabrics, this can cause nausea, headaches, rashes and breathing difficulties.
● Volatile Organic Compounds (VOCs) – found in synthetic foams, these can affect breathing, increase the risk of allergies, cancers and adverse neurological and reproductive effects.

Inexpensive leather sofas are a particular problem. Whilst they appear to be incredible value, they are upholstered in a fabric called bi-cast leather, which is formed by laminating very small pieces of leather onto a vinyl backing sheet. There are two problems with this method: firstly the vinyl backing is likely to

OPPOSITE Simply designed, neutral-coloured sofas have long-lasting appeal and can be seasonally redressed to suit, making it a more sustainable choice. The harder lines of this sofa are softened with feather-filled cushions and the use of decorative natural items on the table.

LEFT The carefully constructed patchwork-fabric covering of this elegant lounger gives it the welcoming feel of a much-loved 'favourite armchair', and if it were to get damaged, well just add another patch. Making furniture easy to repair is an important aspect of sustainability.

contain phthalates, a known toxin on the above list, and secondly whilst it looks like a nice leather sofa, it has no durability – as soon as it receives a deep scratch or tear it is not possible to repair it, as you could if it were 'solid' leather.

When choosing a sofa, the key is durability:
⬤ Durability of materials – it should be solid and well made, with the timber frame coming from a sustainable source. Removable covers mean that if the old ones become worn or damaged they can easily be replaced or repaired. Real leather also softens and improves with age, whilst being easy to clean.
⬤ Durability of design – a simple classic design sofa will not go out of fashion quickly. Choose one in a neutral colour and seasonally redress it with throws or cushions. If you choose a sofa in a bright colour or heavy pattern, it is likely to age more quickly as your tastes and fashions change.

Alternatively, buy vintage or second-hand furniture – if it has contained toxins, it is more likely to have off-gassed already or may even predate the laws governing the use of flame retardants (since 1988 in the UK). Particular favourites of mine are vintage leather sofas. A natural material, leather improves with age, bringing a character to the home that is not precious, but warm and welcoming. Vintage furniture can be easy to live with, settling into your home more naturally and creating a softer overall feel. It is like the difference between your favourite pair of old jeans and a starchy new pair – some things are just better when they are a little worn. Otherwise, opt for a vintage fabric sofa and either have it entirely recovered or cover the removable cushions in several different fabrics for a relaxed mix-and-match feel. If not, removable covers can simply be cleaned, remade or even dyed a darker colour for a cost-effective transformation.

COFFEE TABLES AND SIDE TABLES

Smaller tables have the effect of softening the harder edges of other furniture in a living room; sitting next to a sofa, a coffee table provides a visual step down in height. A coffee table provides surfaces for both decorative and functional objects, whilst side tables allow the convenient positioning of low-energy side lights. By helping to create a fore, middle and background, small tables placed in the centre of the room also have the unexpected visual effect of actually making the room feel bigger.

See them as an additional opportunity to bring the urban eco chic balance of technology, nature and vintage into your living room. I find the idea of creating the perfect side or coffee table extremely exciting; Because it is less functional than a chair or a conventional table you can be even more creative. Be inspired by the following:

TECHNOLOGY

◉ Use a section of recycled plastic sheeting – mottled white surfaces will also help to reflect light into the room, and combine it with some vintage chrome table legs.

◉ Use a recycled glass surface – it may be pricey but it will be a real talking point; you could combine this with old timber fruit boxes for an exciting textural contrast. Views through the glass will show off the weathered boxes.

NATURE

🍂 If you are buying new timber side tables. check that it comes from a sustainable, FSC-certified timber source.

🍂 Go to a timber cutting yard for a section of tree slice with the bark left on. Use a natural oil or wax to finish it and to bring out the texture of the grain.

VINTAGE

❋ Search markets, antique stores or online auction sites for antique or vintage tables – these will add a sense of the sophisticated urban eco chic to your home.

❋ Re-finish an old table by painting it, applying wallpaper to it or even decorating it with mosaic tiles to cover the surface – this can be a relatively simple but exceptionally satisfying project.

OPPOSITE This charismatic living room relies heavily on the vintage to add character, which could be overpowering if weren't for the roughly hewn oak table, which adds a sensual yet contemporary feel.

LEFT The geometric lines of this natural wood floor offset the clean circular form of the table, creating a contemporary Scandinavian aesthetic.

APPLIANCES

The modern living room is filled with technology, from stereos to televisions, DVD players, satellite boxes and games consoles. This presents three problems. Firstly your potential energy usage may be very high, so look for low-energy appliances and ensure they are all turned off when not in use. Secondly this amount of technology leads to a lot of visual clutter, from an array of shiny fascias, buttons and plugs, to miles of cabling. Lastly where does it all go when it becomes obsolete?

It is all too easy to turn off the television from the remote control, but appliances left on standby can still use a wasteful 70% of the energy they consume when on. Either make it a habit to turn everything off at the switch before leaving the room or use an energy-saving mains controller device, which turns off all the items plugged into it using a single infrared switch. Yes it is technology for the lazy, but if it saves energy and money, then it works.

The technology in your living room can be a distraction from what should be a relaxing, social space – it is a form of everyday visual pollution. Why not reveal the technology when you want to use it, but conceal it when you do not. Look for specially designed units that conceal televisions and all their associated technology. Alternatively, scour markets or online auction sites for vintage cabinets or small wardrobes that may be converted into technology cabinets by simply removing sections of the back to allow for ventilation or any elements of the television that extend outwards. Depending on its style, this option may blend more seamlessly into your living space. Or why

not consider adapting an existing cabinet to fit in with the your home's decor. Paint it, wallpaper it, apply goldleaf to it, stencil it or simply change the handles for a more personal feel.

As technology develops, television screens get ever bigger, become more difficult to conceal and simultaneously use more energy. A recent report calculated that for the relative size of screen to the energy used, a video projector

onto a screen or a wall is the most efficient form of viewing. In my home I have installed a video projection system with cables set into the wall from the set top box to the projector. The speakers are concealed in the ceiling and all electrical items are stored out of the way in a low-level plinth that runs the length of the room. This design highlights the fireplace and creates a seating area either side of the hearth, leaving the room free of clutter – whilst allowing for a whopping 1.5m television screen when it is wanted.

The advancing pace of technology is frightening. As soon as you have read through the instruction booklet for your new television, it is out of date. When upgrading, consider recycling the old appliances. Donate items to local charities, sell them on through online auction sites or local papers or swap them via community sites.

ABOVE Combining technology with vintage can add another dimension to appliances. This television on its wheeled base need not be the permanent focal point of a living room – it can be wheeled away into a closet or corner.

THROWS AND BLANKETS

Throws really serve two purposes in your living room; firstly to soften the harder lines of your furniture, making it look more inviting and helping to coordinate it with the space – think of them as a form of decorative layering which you can add to your living room. Secondly and more environmentally friendly, they will keep you warm as you curl up to read or watch TV. As one of the spaces in your home that is not defined by energetic activity, a blanket in your living room will allow you to turn down the heating a little and still stay nice and cosy, having the dual benefit of helping to cut your carbon emissions, and lower your heating bill.

The blanket or throw can also be made of an environmentally conscious material that would have a reduced impact in its production and in terms of the chemicals that it may bring into your home. Think about using natural organic sheep's wool blankets – undyed is best, being available in creams, greys and dark browns. Alternatively but with potentially a larger carbon footprint (and a higher price) you could choose a wonderfully soft alpaca throw, created from smallholding farms in South America (see page 81).

For a recycled fabric option, look into check-patterned wool blankets made from reclaimed wool jumpers and offcuts, although the tartan style look may not be to your taste. Alternatively scour markets for old wool blankets or homely patchwork throws that may just need a good clean. If that all sounds a little too frilly and delicate for you, my personal favourite pastime is searching army surplus stores for old military blankets that are generally available in shades of utilitarian grey. If they are pure wool and have been washed a number of times, they may have shrunk a little, giving them extra thickness and a felt-like quality. I just cannot resist them and have stacks at home, perfect for winter evenings or even hardwearing enough for summer picnics and camping.

CUSHIONS

Adding cushions to your sofas and armchairs adds extra depth and warmth to their appearance – often I think a chair just is not quite complete without one. If chosen right the colours of the cushion will offset that of the upholstery and will soften the harder lines of the furniture. Being made of small sections of fabric means that there is a plethora of recycled fabric cushions out there that are the staple income of many a designer/maker. There are some beautiful cushions and if you want to support local trade and creativity it is worth checking out local art and design fairs or exhibitions for a unique piece.

Alternatively why not try making some yourself; after all it is only a square of fabric cut and sewn to the right size – how difficult can it be? It can be pretty easy and it is a very satisfying little project made even better when friends come round and admire your handiwork. Cushions made from vintage silk (or nylon) headscarves make for a unique and stylish look – be sure to group colours or patterns together for a coordinated effect. If you want a warm familiar feel to your sofa, then why not start by using your old unworn jumpers and sewing them up to accept and hold a cushion pad. If you are after something a little more professionally made, there are plenty of good

materials to choose from such as organic cotton, felt, and super-soft alpaca. Some designers have really gone to town and made them out of hardwearing, factory waste woven seatbelt webbing, and even vintage shirts and ties. So there really is no end to the creativity that could be put into these pieces.

To add a more relaxed and laid-back feel to your lounge, using larger floor cushions on top of a soft surface such as a rug will allow a little more flexibility to the seating of your space.

OPPOSITE These cushions and throws soften the stronger lines of the sofas, adding to their comfort and appeal.

ABOVE This well-worn leather armchair is given a final inviting touch with a soft, feather-filled cushion and wool throw.

WALL HANGINGS

Seize the opportunity to add character to your walls; do not be limited to pictures in frames and mirrors. Consider hanging objects that reflect your passions, whether they be antique fishing rods, vintage handbags or your teenage record collection. Be inventive and search out objects that tell the story of who you are. Look for early samples, quirky examples and unusual artefacts when you are travelling abroad. Collections of objects are perennially fascinating and add character to a space.

That said, framed pictures connect you to your family and past experiences, making a house feel more like a home. There is now an increasing range of picture frames made from reclaimed materials, such as teak, and byproducts of other industries, such as mango wood, bone and mother-of-pearl, which would otherwise be discarded. These are often supplementary industries that spring up in developing countries – they can help local communities become increasingly self-sufficient. Although many are uncertified, these industries often operate under fairtrade principles, but ask exactly what these are.

Of course there is also the vintage option and there is wide availability of old picture frames at markets, second-hand stores and antique shops. Coordinate them by painting them in similar shades or the same as your wall colour.

OPPOSITE This room successfully blends the natural and vintage aspects of urban eco chic; the contemporary artwork gives this living room a vital modern edge, adding real vibrancy and energy.

PLANTS AND FLOWERS

Plants add an often much-needed burst of natural colour to a living room. Displaying nature is a great way to stay in touch with the seasons, providing you do not buy flowers that have been air-freighted from overseas. Instead of high-impact imported blooms, consider displaying small branches of blossom, berries and hand-picked flowers from your garden. Added to which, a number of plants can be very effective at soaking up toxins and CO_2 in the environment – whilst releasing oxygen. Plants such as Chinese evergreen, peace lilies, spider plants, aspidistra, lady palm, bamboo palms, Boston ferns, chrysanthemums and gerbera are all excellent air purifiers, but will need varying degrees of light and water to live.

ECO VASES

There is a good variety of recycled glass vases available, from everyday cylindrical ones to adventurous pieces. But a glass vase does not need to be big to display its eco credentials. Dutch designer Tord Boontje with his partner Emma Woofenden has created a beautiful set of vases made from cut and frosted wine bottles. Manufactured by a Guatemalan co-operative aimed at getting artisans off the street and back into work, they are part of the Design with Conscience Campaign. Whilst not very big they hold a simple stem or a few flowers.

Alternatively, search out collections of vintage glass or pottery vases. Multiples or groupings of complementary shapes and colours will give older designs a new lease of life in your home.

HOME OFFICE

OUR RELIANCE ON TECHNOLOGY TO CONNECT US TO THE WORLD HAS LED THE PERSONAL COMPUTER TO BECOME ONE MORE FIXTURE SQUEEZED INTO OUR HOMES. WHETHER IT IS TO WORK FROM HOME, STAY IN CONTACT WITH FRIENDS OR TO PLAY GAMES, THE HOME OFFICE LOOKS SET TO STAY.

A home office increases the pressure on your personal space, but also offers environmental benefits. Not only does it allow you to work from home, thereby avoiding unnecessary journeys into the office, it makes a whole tranche of information readily accessible so that you can thoroughly research the key decisions you need to make in your life. Making informed choices helps to reduce your carbon footprint: finding local suppliers, researching toxins, investigating sustainable alternatives and energy savings.

Your home office may be a dedicated room, shared room, the guest room, or space in another room that is large enough to house all the necessary technology. Wherever you locate your office, make a positive effort to create a happy, healthy place to work; you will benefit from it physically, mentally and creatively. Ventilate the space properly; ensure windows can be opened for fresh air. Plants bring vibrancy and energy, plus they help to clean the air, and consider using scented candles, which can create a calmer working environment.

But how can creating a balance between the principles of technology, nature and vintage help you to create a better workspace? Technology is key to the home office. It provides not just efficient-energy reducing machines and lighting, but also better communication systems that reduce your need to travel. It can also help you to cut down on resources such as paper by storing information rather than having to print it out. From a materials point of view, it can create a fresh, bright and dust-reducing space that will be better for you and the technology that you are using.

OPPOSITE A home office space can be incorporated into any room and can be as simple as a trestle table, comfortable chairs and adequate task lighting.

Nature has a grounding influence in the workspace. The textural quality of natural materials will limit the build-up of the contributors to sick building syndrome, such as static electricity, and help you to relax at work by reducing stress. Nature also helps to lower the level of toxins in the air through the use of VOC-free paints and plants, which make a space feel vibrant and more alive.

Vintage items can help you to feel relaxed, comfortable and inspired. This is a great space to make small collections of objects that capture your imagination, no matter how diverse they are from your actual day-to-day work. Using vintage furniture in your home office, such as an antique desk chair or lamp, creates textural contrasts in the space that will be more exciting and help to create a relaxed feeling – a world away from uptight corporate boardrooms with twenty of the same chair regimented around a large meeting table.

WALLS

Use paler shades throughout your workspace to keep it feeling fresh and to bounce natural light around, but being an office you may also wish to paint the space either above or behind your desk with a vibrant energy-boosting colour. Natural paints are available in a wide range of colours, so it is now possible to find bold shades that will not bring toxic VOCs into your home. Take inspiration from the vibrant natural greens of spring or the warm autumnal shades of orange. You may want to pin up inspirational images or even spreadsheets on your walls – to do this, use recycled newspaper pulp pin-up board called Sundela, which is strong but soft enough to push in drawing pins.

RIGHT Good storage adds real flexibility to the home office, allowing all your private papers to be quickly and neatly tidied away and leaving the room free to be used for other functions, such as a guest bedroom.

FURNITURE

If your home office is a shared space, flexibility is key. You may want to invest in a fold-up or sofa bed if using your spare bedroom, which allows you to maximise on office space when no guests are staying. In addition you may want to find ways of closing up your desk area when you do have guests, so they can relax without feeling as if they are prying into your affairs. A built-in workspace with hinged or sliding doors could be the answer, but may require a cabinetmaker to construct it.

If your study is a limited area within a larger space, pack it away. Psychologically this is important – when your working hours are over, your desk and anything unfinished remain out of sight. Transform an armoire into a study cupboard, creating something unique from an antique cabinet. Source sliding brackets and hinges from hardware stores and ensure the heights of any surfaces are correct by copying the dimensions of an existing comfortable desk.

WORK DESKS

Depending on your office space, your desk size may vary greatly. If you have the luxury of a dedicated room, then the desk could be of a standard size but made of different materials:
● TECHNOLOGY – use recycled plastic sheeting to create a sleek surface, fixing legs or trestles for a simple, industrial aesthetic.
NATURE – buy or make a timber desk that uses FSC certified timber.
VINTAGE – reclaim an old steel or timber desk and make it your own. Strip steel down to the bare metal for a retro feel, whilst timber bureaus can be stripped, stained or painted.

DESK CHAIRS

It is a sad reality that one of the most common complaints of those working at home is the increase in repetitive strain injury (RSI). Using the right office chair rather than simply any old kitchen chair can combat this.

The office chair has moved on a long way recently; a number of manufacturers are taking seriously the issues of ergonomics and sustainability. Desk chairs are now fully flexible, with adjustments in seat height, armrests and back support – creating a better, healthier seating position with total support for the spine. From a sustainability perspective, some office chairs are manufactured with a high recycled material content and are being designed with a minimal number of parts – which are easy to disassemble in as little as five minutes – up to 99% of which can then be recycled. It is now possible to choose a desk chair that is better for you, whilst being beautiful to look at and caring of the environment.

But a home office is not only a space for sitting at a desk, typing away. You may want to create a relaxed seating area as well, offering a quiet space to take a welcome break from the computer. The addition of a comfortable armchair goes a long way in creating a more welcoming work environment. Whilst you could look for some slouchy seating or even a beanbag, a vintage armchair will add a homely but textural element, contrasting with and softening the harder edges of a more dynamic technology-filled workspace. If you have the space, it is a luxury well worth considering.

SHELVING AND STORAGE

Good storage is essential for a clutter-free workspace, keeping what you need to hand but without visually polluting your office. You should consider immediate storage for pieces that you use everyday such as pens, pencils, paper; medium-term storage for occasional items such as books and files; and long-term storage for anything used only every so often.

Storage can take the form of built-in shelves, cabinets or freestanding units. In addition, make room for the display of those items that inspire you. It may seem whimsical but these objects or collections are aide-mémoires, reminding you of who you are and your passions. They bring a touch of inspirational nature or vintage into your workspace.

LEFT Industrial metal shelving makes a stylish storage option for a home office, especially if you soften the harsher edges of the steel with your personal collections of books and memorabilia.

ABOVE A minimal all-white office has been cleverly fitted into the corner of a spare room by using a shaped desk. The wall -mounted plastic storage unit keeps everything in its place and the worksurface uncluttered.

REDUCE AND RECYCLE

By using all that technology has to offer, you can create a more efficient workspace – one that uses less electricity and other resources, such as paper. As you work, ensure that you:

◉ Turn off all appliances when you finish for the day. You can now purchase special plugs that will automatically turn off all other appliances when you switch off your computer.

◉ Make the most of communication technologies, such as digital imaging, conference calling and broadband, in order to reduce the need for travel and posting items.

◉ Use recycled paper in your printer.

◉ Print on both sides of paper (though you may need a thicker grade of paper to do this).

◉ Keep two bins – one for conventional rubbish and one specifically for paper and envelopes – this also makes paper easier to reuse, providing you do not crush it up.

◉ Recycle your empty printer cartridges – they are valuable to others.

◉ Recycle obsolete items of IT – look online for charities that will take old computers and printers away for use in schools or developing countries or for local community groups, such as freecycle.org. If it is totally out of date, contact your local authority who can advise how best to dispose of any items without sending them to landfill.

OPPOSITE Plants can do a lot for the home office environment. A direct link to nature, the colour and scent of a plant enlivens the atmosphere of a workspace. Research has shown that plants can help to lower your blood pressure and stress levels, increase productivity and remove airborne toxins that can leak from plastics, MDF, computers and printers, as well as absorbing carbon dioxide and emitting oxygen, creating an enlivening and concentration-boosting breath of fresh air.

LIGHTING

Good lighting is key for a task-heavy area, such as a workspace. Whilst utilising all available natural daylight to avoid using electrical lighting, you will need to reduce any glare from the sun and reflectance on your screen, which can make computer work uncomfortable. So as well as increasing the natural or reflected light into the space (see pages 16 and 32), you may also want to fit windows with solar shading devices. Consider conventional or Venetian blinds, which can easily be adjusted depending on the time of day and angle of the sun.

For general lighting, aim for an even spread of lights across the room. A consistent level of illumination makes a room safer to move around and eases eye strain, as you do not have to focus from light to dark areas. A single pendant bulb or ceiling-mounted spotlights with low-energy bulbs may suffice, but it is likely your desk will be positioned against a wall, throwing shadows onto your desk and keyboard. A better solution is to install a spread of low-energy LED spotlights across the ceiling. This will give you an even array of general light as well as direct task light over your desk area.

To create the right level of illumination onto your desk, you may need an additional task light, such as an anglepoise or desk lamp. Choose one with a sufficient shade to reduce the impact of any glare on your eyes and that has a good level of built-in flexibility, making it as adjustable as possible. This could be as elegant as a classic anglepoise lamp or as understated as a New-York-style loft lamp. However, there is also a new generation of LED or low-energy fluorescent task lights available.

ENTRANCES AND HALLWAYS

ENTRANCES AND CONNECTING SPACES ARE OFTEN NEGLECTED, BUT OFFER A KEY OPPORTUNITY TO MAKE A HOME FEEL COHESIVE, VIBRANT AND LOVED. MANY CULTURES REVERE THE HOME'S THRESHOLD – REGARDING IT AS A SYMBOL OF POWER, WEALTH AND A SACRED SPACE – AND DECORATE ENTRANCES WITH ORNATE METAL WORK, CARVINGS OR FLOWERS.

BELOW It is possible to inject personality and humour into even the smallest of spaces. I love this quirky coat hook feature; it is both a functional and creative statement.

RIGHT Hallways serve more purposes than you may think, so multi-functional spaces like this add warmth and character whilst allowing you to get your coat and shoes on, and check yourself in the mirror, before leaving the house.

From even a basic, plain front door we make assumptions about the sorts of people who live within that home. Based on first impressions we can often surmise whether they are house proud, diy enthusiasts, have children, keep pets, prefer a tidy home or maybe live in organised chaos. First impressions do count, and if you want to portray a sense of who you are, this is the most public place to do it.

From a practical point of view, front doors and hallways act as a barrier and buffer to the environment beyond; providing security, light and insulation to the cold or heat. It is also worth remembering that draughts account for on average 15% of the heat loss in our houses. As with any space in the home, we need to combine practicality, style and environmental awareness to create a hallway that truly represents you as a follower of urban eco chic.

A balance can be found between the use of technology, nature and vintage in entrances and hallways. The use of technology adds warmth through insulation and draught exclusion in doors and windows, and thermostatic valves keep radiators at a regular temperature – all reducing your energy consumption. The careful use of glass will allow light to filter through into the space, reducing the need for electrical usage.

Using nature benefits hallways with hardwearing materials that can withstand heavy traffic and at the same time demonstrate your passion for the environment. Whilst the use of vintage can impart identity and individuality to even the smallest space and, if you use an antique mirror, subtly bounce light around.

DOORS

Fitting a new door will improve your home security, cut draughts blowing through each room and give the facade a facelift. A number of manufacturers can design, make and fit a new front door in either traditional or contemporary styles. Ensure that any new door:

- Uses timber from an FSC-certified source.
- Uses sealed double glazed units for any glass.
- Complies with all building regulations.
- Incorporates integral draught control.
- Uses recyclable door furniture (stainless steel).
- Uses locks that meet all required standards.

However, if you do not want a new or period, style front door, there is always the vintage option. Carefully note the key measurements of your door, then take a trip to your local reclamation yard; they are likely to have the door types prevalent in your area. Check for any warps or splits in the timber and cracks in glazing panels. If you cannot find a door that is an exact fit, buy one that is marginally larger so it can be trimmed down. But go cautiously – take too much off and you may ruin the structure of the woodwork. As doors are heavy and need precise fitting, this may be best carried out by an experienced carpenter.

As a designer I have a deep dislike of moulded uPVC doors that pastiche period styles. Whilst it can be strong and insulating, uPVC is a harmful material to create. It visually degrades as it ages and it is non-degradable and difficult to recycle. On top of all this, to me uPVC doors look cheap and so I would always seek a timber alternative and fit draught excluders and covers to the locks and letter box.

LIGHTING

Even when rooms are light and airy, the spaces that link them can feel dark and lifeless. As hallways are often long corridors with only small sources of natural light, electrical lighting will be called upon daily. To reduce your energy bills and CO_2, you have to work hard at finding ways to allow as much light as possible to filter into these spaces. Your efforts will be worth it – as well as reducing your need for electricity, your hallways will come to life, feeling lighter and more vibrant. To keep your hallway light, consider the following:

● Paint walls in light-reflective shades.
● Paint window frames and sills in light shades so they bounce daylight straight in.
● Keep windows clean and unobstructed.
● Do not obscure windows with heavy drapes.
● Fit opaque or frosted glass panels into doors leading from rooms with windows.
● Fit roof lights or a solar light tube to bring light from the roof down to the hallway.
● Use toughened glass in balustrades and even stairs to filter light down from above.
● If your home has more than one floor, fit an upper-level hallway with an opaque structural glass floor panel to filter light down.
● Fit automatic switches, limiting the time lights are left on. These can take the form of infra-red movement-detecting (PIR) switches which can activate lighting from just a few seconds to several minutes. They can also be adjusted to activate only once darkness falls, so will not operate during the daytime light.
● Use light-reflective flooring, such as timber or ceramic tiles.
● Hang vintage mirrors on hallway walls to bounce light in and through the space.

STORAGE

With the increasing demands on our homes to incorporate more and more functions, it is sometimes difficult to keep our homes and hallways clear of clutter. But a home with blocked passageways will exert an unseen yet suffocating pressure on your life. Squeezing past shoes, coats, recycling boxes and even bikes will make entering, leaving and moving around your home stressful. It is up to you to put in place a system that makes your hallway a tidy fluid space that is a pleasure to use and clear enough to say a little about who you are to visitors entering for the first time, but consider the following:

● Find a space, be it a table, or hook that you can put your keys on. Keep it out of sight of the front door to stop burglars reaching in and lifting them.
● Use bulldog clips screwed to the wall to hold mail and keep tabletops clear.
● Find spaces for recycling boxes, such as under the stairs, or build racks for them so they stack neatly out the way.
● Fix a hook on the back of your front door and hang a reusable shopping bag there so you remember it whenever you leave home.
● Ban coats from the hallway; they build up over time and are annoying to squeeze past.
● Hang your bike by a wall or ceiling hook if you must have it inside, so at least it is out the way and will not fall over.
● Make the most of all concealed 'Cinderella spaces' for storing shoes or storage boxes. If the space under the stairs has not been touched for six months, clear it out and use it for storing items you use on a daily and weekly basis like recycling bins.

ABOVE A successful balance of the urban eco chic principles of technology, nature and vintage has been created here between the multi-striped stair runner, the rustic timber table and the vintage telephone, creating a fresh harmonious feel.

ECO RESOURCES

ECO INFORMATION

ACT ON CO$_2$
actonco2.direct.gov.uk
*a government site where
you can calculate your
carbon footprint and get
advice on how to cut your
carbon emissions*

COOL EARTH
coolearth.org
*a charity that protects
endangered rainforest to
combat global warming,
protect ecosystems and
provide sustainable jobs*

ENERGY SAVING TRUST
energysavingtrust.org.uk
*free impartial advice on how
to cut back your CO$_2$
emissions, including a
home energy report and
information on energy-
saving products*

RECYCLING SERVICES

COMMUNITY REPAINT
communityrepaint.org.uk
*donate any unwanted
reusable paint to help local
communities and individuals*

RECYCLE NOW
recyclenow.com
*a one-stop recycling
information centre including
Recycling Made Easy video
with Oliver Heath*

[RE]DESIGN
redesigndesign.org
*a social enterprise that
promotes sustainability in
product design*

ECO HOMES

GREEN MOVES
greenmoves.co.uk
*online estate agent for
eco-friendly property*

ENERGY EFFICIENCY

**CAVITY INSULATION
GUARANTEE AGENCY**
ciga.co.uk
*independent agency
providing guarantees for
cavity wall insulation fitted
by registered installers*

**LOW CARBON BUILDINGS
PROGRAMME**
lowcarbonbuildings.org.uk
*government programme
providing grants for
installing certified energy-
saving products*

ECO BUILDING MATERIALS

**FOREST STEWARDSHIP
COUNCIL**
fsc.org
*independent, non-profit
organisation to promote the
responsible management of
the world's forests*

GREEN BUILDING STORE
greenbuildingstore.co.uk
T 08700 119 899
*online store for green
building products including
natural paints, sheep's wool
insulation and FSC-certified
timber products*

GREENSPEC
greenspec.co.uk
*guide to green building
products and materials*

ECO FLOORS

COMPLETELY FLOORING
completelyflooring.co.uk
T 08700 119 899
linoleum and bamboo

INTERFACE
interfaceflor.eu
T 01274 690 690
*ethically produced
sustainable carpet tiles*

**JAYMART RUBBER &
PLASTICS LTD**
jaymart.net
T 01373 864 926
*flooring made from recycled
rubber bus and truck tyres*

RECLAIMED TIMBER
reclaimed.uk.com
T 020 8558 2811
recycled timber flooring

SIESTA CORK TILES
siestacorktiles.co.uk
T 020 8683 4055
cork floor and wall tiles

**THE ALTERNATIVE
FLOORING COMPANY**
alternativeflooring.com
T 01264 335 111
*coir, jute, sisal, pure wool
and wool blends*

WICANDER
wicanders.com
T 01403 710 001
cork and rubber mix floors

ECO WALLS

CALCH TY-MAWR LIME
lime.org.uk
*centre for traditional and
ecological building including
lime plaster, eco paints and
sheep's wool insulation*

EARTHBORN PAINTS
earthbornpaints.co.uk
T 01928 734 171
*eco paints in shades
designed by Oliver Heath*

LIME TECHNOLOGY LTD
limetechnology.co.uk
*lime-based building products
including lime plaster*

LOUISE BODY WALLPRINT
louisebodywallprint.com
T 07734 907 357
eco-friendly wallpapers

SILVA TIMBER PRODUCTS
silvatimber.co.uk
T 0151 495 3331
timber cladding

ECO SURFACES

CORIAN
corian.co.uk
T 0800 962 116
*surfaces and sinks for
kitchens and bathrooms*

DURAT
durat.com
T 0358 (0)2 252 1000
recycled plastics

EIGHT INCH
eightinch.co.uk
T 01273 511 564
*Resilica recycled crushed
glass set in ecoresin*

ELUNA
eluna.org.uk
T 020 7241 7485
recycled glass tiles

GREENHOUSE EFFECT
greenhouseeffect.co.uk
T 01323 871 399
*100% recycled glass for
kitchens and bathrooms*

SMILE PLASTICS
smile-plastics.co.uk
T 01743 850 267
*recycled plastic sheets
made from waste products
including mobiles and wellies*

3 FORM
3-form.com
T +1 212 627 0883
*ecoresin panels with
encapsulated reeds,
grasses and other items*

ECO LIGHTING

ECOCENTRIC
ecocentric.co.uk
T 020 7739 3888
*energy-saving lightbulbs,
stylish low-energy lighting
including LED chandeliers
and fairy lights, and 100%
organic plant wax candles*

LUMOS LIGHTING
lumoslighting.co.uk
T 0191 281 5050
LED lighting

MADELEINE BOULESTEIX
madeleineboulesteix.co.uk
T 020 7737 8171
*ornate chandeliers made
from discarded materials
including teacups, cutlery
and jelly moulds*

MEGAMAN ENERGY
SAVING LAMPS
megamanuk.com
T 0845 408 4625
low-energy bulbs

SOLATUBE
T 0845 458 0101
solalighting.co.uk
low-energy sun tubes

ECO KITCHENS

BLANCO
blanco.co.uk
*stainless steel kitchen sinks
with recycled content*

ECO INTERIORS
ecointeriors-uk.com
T 020 7737 8110
*ecological and sustainable
kitchens and other furniture*

MILESTONE ECO DESIGN
milestone.uk.net
T 0845 457 7153
*specialists in kitchens of
recycled content, including
recycled plastic kitchen units
made from yoghurt pots*

NEIL LERNER
neillerner.com
T 020 7433 0705
*bespoke kitchen design,
including bamboo units*

QUOOKER
quooker.com
*the boiling water tap
providing instant hot water*

ECO BATHROOMS

HANSGROHE
hansgrohe.co.uk
T 01372 465 655
*water-saving bathroom
fittings including grey water
recycling systems and eco
smart showers*

ROCA
roca-uk.com
T 01530 830 080
*water-saving cisterns, taps,
flow restrictors and valves*

TAPMAGIC
tapmagic.co.uk
T 0845 652 5458
*water-saving units that
convert flow to spray, which
can be retrofitted to all taps*

ECO FURNITURE

JIMMIE MARTIN LTD
jimmiemartin.com
T 020 7033 9507
*reupholstered and
decorated furniture from
design duo Jimmie Karlsson
and Martin Nihlmar*

PIET HEIN EEK
pietheineek.com
T +31 40 285 6610
*reclaimed scrapwood
furniture from Dutch
designer Piet Hein Eek*

SQUINT
squintlimited.com
T 020 7739 9275
*Lisa Whatmough's exquisite
patchwork furniture*

ECO FABRICS

ANNIE SHERBOURNE
anniesherburne.co.uk
T 020 7328 2182
*ecological yarn and textiles
including felt*

ECOCENTRIC
ecocentric.co.uk
T 020 7739 3888
*organic cotton bed linen,
organic alpaca and felt
cushions, pure wool throws*

HELEN AMY MURRAY
helenamymurray.com
T 020 8533 0669
*bespoke upholstery and
wall treatments in leather*

HEMP SHOP
thehempshop.co.uk
T 0845 123 5869
*hemp and hemp blend
fabrics in all weights*

FABRICATIONS
fabrications1.co.uk
T 020 7275 8043
*cushions made from
recycled materials including
shirts and ties*

INGEO
ingeofibers.com
T +1 952 742 0400
starch polymers

NAISH
naishfelts.co.uk
T 01722 743 505

ECO GADGETS

BYE BYE STANDBY
byebyestandby.co.uk
T 0845 833 3803
*'smart extensions' that turn
off up to four appliances
saving energy and money*

DIY KYOTO
diykyoto.com
T 01738 447 741
*award-winning device that
measures and displays
domestic electricity usage*

EWGECO
ewgeco.com
T 01738 447 741
*management system that
measures and displays
household energy usage*

PICTURE CREDITS

The publisher has made every effort to trace the copyright holders. We apologise in advance for any unintentional omission and would be pleased to insert the appropriate acknowledgement in any subsequent edition.

2 Pernille Howalt/House of Pictures/styling Pernille Lykke; 9 Paul Massey/Living etc/IPC+ Syndication; 10–11 Istock; 12 Lars Ranek; 15 Marie Claire Maison/Mai-Linh/Box Managment/C.ARDOUIN/Stylist Roxane BEIS home; 19 Simon Scarboro/reproduced from House Beautiful Magazine/National Magazine Company/Retna UK; 22–3 Sharyn Cairns/Tuckey House; 24–5 Axolotl Group; 27 Ray Main/Mainstreamimages/ Oliver Heath Design; 39 Ray Main/Mainstreamimages; 42 Sharyn Cairns/Tuckey House; 44–5 Formica® Metallics - Copper Treadworks Formica Ltd; 46 Louise Body louisebodywallprint.com; 50–1 Ray Main/Mainstreamimages/Oliver Heath Design; 53 above left Ray Main/Mainstreamimages/Oliver Heath Design; 53 above right Bamboo Flooring Company; 53 centre left Dalsouple; 53 centre right siestacorktiles.co.uk; 53 below left Hemp Fabric UK; 53 below right siestacorktiles.co.uk; 55 Mikkel Strange/Linnea Press/styling Jesper Grand; 56 Ray Main/ Mainstreamimages; 59 © Narratives/Polly Wreford; 60 left Andreas von Einsiedel/interior design by Clare Lattin and Mark Hix; 60 right Henry Wilson/Redcover.com; 63 above left Martine Hamilton Knight/arcaid.co.uk; 63 above right Tom Leighton/Living etc/IPC+ Syndication; 63 centre left © 2005. All rights reserved. Image provided courtesy of 3form, Inc; 63 centre right Louise Body louisebodywallprint.com; 63 below left 100% recycled glass by Eluna; 63 below right Ed Reeve/ Redcover.com; 64–5 Jens Stoltze/Linnea Press/styling Sidsel Zachariasen; 67 Marie Claire Maison/E.BARBE/C.ARDOUIN/ by two architects: W.FEYFERLIK and S.FRITZER; 68 Marie Claire Maison/V.LEROUX/Temps Machine/C.ARDOUIN/Stylist Marthe DESMOULINS home; 71 above right marcusbleyl.com/greenhouseeffect.co.uk; 71 above left Nathalie Krag/ Taverne Agency/styled and produced by Tami Christiansen; 71 centre left Ray Main/Mainstreamimages/Oliver Heath Design; 71 centre right Istock; 71 below left photo courtesy of Smith and Fong Plyboo; 71 below right Gary Nicholson – Eight Inch Ltd; 73 above Ray Main/Mainstreamimages/Oliver Heath Design; 73 below Gary Nicholson – Eight Inch Ltd; 74 Ray Main/Mainstreamimages/David Gill; 77 above right Ray Main/Mainstreamimages/Oliver Heath Design; 77 above left Annie Sherburne; 77 centre right © EcoCentric; 77 centre left Ray Main/Mainstreamimages/squintlimited.com; 77 below left Marie Claire Maison/Mai-Linh/Box Managment/C.ARDOUIN/Anja and Parry KOOPS home, Balthazar Keuken, Amsterdam; 77 below right © EcoCentric; 79 Nathalie Krag/Taverne Agency/styled and produced by Tami Christiansen; 80 Winfried Heinze/Redcover.com; 83 above Henry Wilson/Redcover.com; 83 below Paul Massey/ Mainstreamimages; 85 above left OXO International and Phillips Provan International as the exclusive distributors; 85 above right Madeleine Boulesteix; 85 centre left Ray Main/Mainstreamimages/Oliver Heath Design; 85 centre right © Hotze Eisma; 85 below left Marie Claire Idées/L.GAILLARD/P.CHASTRES/A.CHATILLON; 85 below right re-foundobjects.com; 87 Mel Yates/Media 10 Images; 88 Lisbett Wedendahl/House of Pictures; 90–1 Istock; 92 Nathalie Krag/Taverne Agency/producer Tami Christiansen; 94 left Marie Claire Maison/V.LEROUX/Temps Machine/C.ARDOUIN/ Jérôme and Anne ISRAEL; 94 right Lars Ranek; 95 Marie Claire Maison/Mai-Linh/Box Managment/C.ARDOUIN/Dana KAPELIAN/Plasticienne; 98 Lars Ranek; 99 Marie Claire Maison/V.LEROUX/Temps Machine; 102 Mikkel Strange/Linnea Press/styling Jesper Grand; 104–5 Marie Claire Maison/V.LEROUX/Temps Machine/C.ARDOUIN/Stylist Marthe DESMOULINS home; 107 © Jefferson Smith/Sarah Wigglesworth Architects; 108 Lars Ranek; 111 Mikkel Adsbøl/Linnea Press/styling Pernille Vest; 112 Bieke Claessens/Redcover.com; 115 Mikkel Vang/Taverne Agency/production Christine Rudolph; 116 left Earl Carter/Taverne Agency/producer Anne Marie Kiely; 116 right Ray Main/Mainstreamimages/ Foundassociates.com; 118 Mike Huibregtse, Manager – Photographic Art, Kohler Co; 119 Mike Huibregtse, Manager – Photographic Art, Kohler Co; 120 Bieke Claessens/Redcover.com; 123 Paul Massey/Living etc/IPC+ Syndication; 124 Paul Massey/Living etc/IPC+ Syndication; 127 Ray Main/Mainstreamimages/Oliver Heath Design; 128–9 Ray Main/ Mainstreamimages/Jura Distillery; 131 Richard Birch/Living etc/IPC+ Syndication; 132 Marie Claire Maison/V.LEROUX/ Temps Machine/C.ARDOUIN/Stylist Marthe DESMOULINS home; 133 Chris Tubbs/Media 10 Images; 135 Debi Treloar/ Redcover.com; 136 Hotze Eisma/Taverne Agency/producer Julia Bird; 137 Marie Claire Maison/Mai-Linh/Box Managment/ C.ARDOUIN/Anja and Parry KOOPS home, Balthazar Keuken, Amsterdam; 138 Alun Callender/Redcover.com; 139 Ray Main/Mainstreamimages/designer Ben De Lisi; 141 Heidi Lerkenfeldt/Linnea Press/styling Pernille Vest; 142 Heidi Lerkenfeldt/Linnea Press/styling Pernille Vest; 143 Heidi Lerkenfeldt/Linnea Press/styling Pernille Vest; 144–5 Ray Main/ Mainstreamimages/squintlimited.com; 146 Edina van der Wyck/Media 10 Images; 148 ewastock.com; 149 Andreas von Einsiedel/interior design by Clare Lattin and Mark Hix; 150 Hotze Eisma/Taverne Agency/producer Julia Bird; 151 Ray Main/Mainstreamimages/squintlimited.com; 152 Graham Atkins Hughes/Redcover.com; 153 Mikkel Adsbøl/Linnea Press/styling Hanne Vind; 154–5 Pernille Howalt/House of Pictures/styling Pernille Lykke; 156 Prue Ruscoe/Taverne Agency/producer Tami Christiansen; 157 Verity Welstead/Redcover.com; 159 Mikkel Adsbøl/Linnea Press/styling Hanne Vind; 161 Marie Claire Maison/Mai-Linh/Box Managment/C.ARDOUIN/Anja and Parry KOOPS home, Balthazar Keuken, Amsterdam; 162 Mikkel Adsbøl/Linnea Press/styling Hanne Vind; 164 Marie Claire Maison/E.BARBE/C.ARDOUIN; 165 Lars Ranek; 166 Mikkel Adsbøl/Linnea Press/styling Hanne Vind; 168 Mikkel Adsbøl/Linnea Press/styling Hanne Vind; 169 Debi Treloar/Redcover.com; 171 Verity Welstead/Living etc/IPC+ Syndication.

The statistics quoted on pages 29–31 were provided by The Energy Saving Trust/energysavingtrust.org.uk.

INDEX

Figures in *italics* refer to captions

ACKNOWLEDGEMENTS

I would like to thank all those people who have given me their time, expertise and help in writing this book. To Nikki Blustin and Sarah Kahn at Blustin Heath Design for their research assistance, suggestions and proofreading. To the team at EcoCentric – Michael, Niki and Leena, who have spent so much time researching products and building the online store, which has influenced my thinking about Urban Eco Chic. Thank you too for all those that gave their time to help me in my research Madeleine Boulestix, who makes such beautiful reclaimed chandeliers; Greta Corke, John Sawdon Smith and Richard Woods at DIY Kyoto who design the most stylish of energy meters; Barley Massey and her wonderful recycled fabric; Jimmie Karlsson and Martin Nihlmar at Jimmie Martin who make their Baroque and Roll furniture; Piet Hein Eek the most stylish reclaimed timber furniture designer ever; Gary Nicholson who creates sparkling recycled glass work surfaces at Eight Inch; and Lisa Whatmough whose patchwork chic furniture at Squint is such an inspiration. And last but not least for all those at my wonderful publishers, Quadrille, who have had listened to my ideas and given them so much well-considered attention. In particular, thank you Jane, Helen, Lisa and Claire.

Deutschsprachige Literatur
in den suhrkamp taschenbüchern:
Lyrik

H. C. Artmann: Gedichte über die Liebe und über die Lasterhaftigkeit.
st 1033

– How much, schatzi? st 136

– ein lilienweißer brief aus lincolnshire. gedichte aus 21 jahren. st 498

The Best of H. C. Artmann. st 275

Jürgen Becker: Gedichte. 1965–1980. st 690

Thomas Brasch: Der schöne 27. September. Gedichte. st 903

Volker Braun: Gedichte. st 499

Bertolt Brecht: Ge...